Fifty Shades of Chicken

Fifty Shades of Chicken

A Parody in a Cookbook

FL Fowler

CLARKSON POTTER/PUBLISHERS
NEW YORK

Copyright © 2012 by FL Fowler

All rights reserved.
Published in the United States by Clarkson Potter/Publishers,
an imprint of the Crown Publishing Group, a division of Random
House, Inc., New York.
www.crownpublishing.com
www.clarksonpotter.com

CLARKSON POTTER is a trademark and POTTER with colophon
is a registered trademark of Random House, Inc.

Library of Congress Cataloging-in-Publication Data is available
upon request.

ISBN 978-0-385-34522-4
eISBN 978-0-385-34523-1

Printed in the United States of America

Design by Stephanie Cluckwork
Photographs by John von Pamer
Cover photography by John von Pamer

10 9 8 7 6 5 4 3 2

First Edition

For chicken lovers everywhere

CONTENTS

INTRODUCTION

How have I gotten myself into this? I glance around the spotless, meticulously organized kitchen: trussing twine, skewers, mallets—is that a *cleaver*? Holy crap.

I don't even fit in. I share a shelf in the fridge with a ham so enormous I have to huddle up against the door, even though it's a double-wide Sub-Zero. The other shelves are stuffed with bags of leafy greens, neatly wrapped paper parcels of what might be fish or fancy cheese, and uniform rows of carefully labeled condiment jars. Down in a crisper all by itself is a radish, aloof and flaunting its freshness. Then there's me, mundane, scrawny, and shrink-wrapped.

I'm closest with the enormous ham, even though she's so much cooler than I am. She hogs the shelf, but she's my nearest, dearest friend. She's piquant, smoky, salty, pigheaded, bodacious, and always seems to know what's cooking. She'll make an exceptional holiday dinner.

SUDDENLY THE FRIDGE DOOR I'm resting on swings open, and I find myself rolling off the shelf and falling toward the kitchen floor. *Crap.* My plastic wrapper bursts as I land, and my giblet bag slides halfway out. *Double crap.* Damn my cheap packaging.

Instantly I feel hands on me, lifting me carefully from the tiles. Long, powerful fingers cradle me from underneath and expertly tuck my giblets back in place. *Holy cow.* Something clenches deep inside me.

My rescuer lays me gently on a countertop. He's wearing jeans and a clean white apron. He's young and handsome, with a rakish mop of hair. He has muscled arms and clearly works out. But it's his hands that have me mesmerized. They're smooth, pale, perfectly manicured, and beyond competent.

The kitchen is all sleek white tile, blonde wood, and black granite. There's no clutter on the shiny counters and the ceramic backsplash is bare, except for an incredibly long magnetic knife rack. It's filled with gray steel blades of all kinds—fat, thin, long, short, curved, and straight, and all of them obviously sharp as hell. Displayed together, they are breathtaking. He notices my attention fixed on them.

"You like my collection?" he asks coolly.

"Extraordinary. Like an artist's tools," I say slowly. He cocks his head to one side, and then to the other. He looks at me in a way that sears my gizzard.

"I couldn't agree more," he replies, his voice suddenly soft, and for some reason I find myself blushing.

"There m-must be four dozen knives up there," I stammer. I'm hypnotized by their gleaming edges and his hands at the same time.

"Fifty blades, to be precise," he intones. "This kitchen is my domain. I need to have complete control when I prep."

Holy shit. The way he says it shakes my liver out of place again. Mr. Blades can prep me any time.

"I can imagine," I manage to say.

"It's all about finesse, Miss Hen." Whoa, he keeps shifting direction. He's so weirdly formal. Who calls a chicken "Miss Hen"? But then nobody's ever really taken the time to talk to me before.

"I have enormous respect for food," he continues. "To derive deep satisfaction from the mundane: tournéing a radish, cutting a potato, portioning a syllabub. These form the foundation of what I do."

"Raising the mundane to the extraordinary," I say, mesmerized. I really shouldn't look at his hands, it's unsettling.

He cocks his head and gazes at me. I blush again under the burning force of that stare. He's cooking me with his eyes. *How does he do that?*

His words continue to echo in the secret darkness of my soul. "It's all about finesse." *Chickens don't do finesse,* my subconscious sneers at me. I flush at my foolish, inward thoughts. But a girl can dream, can't she?

one

The
Novice Bird

He's clearly not into me. I wait quietly on the counter and watch his skillful, knowing hands work. Desire pools way down in my cavity and in spite of myself I start to daydream while he preps a radish.

He cocks an eyebrow. "Penny for your thoughts, Miss Hen?" He appears focused on his task, but there's a sly glint in his eye.

I flush. *Oh, I was just imagining your hands traveling up my thighs and your teeth nibbling my breast.*

"You seem to have a lot of little bowls," I say as calmly as possible.

He has arranged a dozen tiny ramekins in an orderly row on the counter. He fills each of them with a spice, an herb, or a chopped ingredient carefully portioned from a measuring spoon.

"You're a very sharp-eyed chicken," he says, and that look returns. "I exercise perfect control over everything that happens in this kitchen. I require exactitude from my ingredients."

What a control freak. And arrogant to boot. But the apron he's wearing hangs off his hips in a way that turns my bones to jelly.

"So, what are you whipping up there?" I ask hopefully.

"Well, what I'm 'whipping up,' as you put it, is a *salade composé*," he says without a trace of humor in his smile. "I create experiences. It's my belief that a meal can be a transcendent experience, like a Bach concerto. It's all about finesse. I know what makes ingredients tick. I find the best ones, and then take them beyond themselves. The bottom line is that it always comes down to ingredients that know what I want." He stares at me intently.

Why does he have such an unnerving effect on me? He's constantly shifting. One minute he's all foxy looks and hungry smiles, the next he's curt and sharp. His fridge is packed with exotic foods, but he seems to have eyes only for the radish. *Could it be?*

"Are you a vegetarian?" I blurt before I can stop myself.

He draws a sharp breath. I am mortified beyond words. *Double crap.* Why can't I keep my head on for once? My agonized subconscious is begging me on bended knee to stop gabbling.

"No, Chicken, I'm not." He cocks his head to one side and stares coolly at me. He is not amused. I cringe. I feel the blood drain from my entire body.

"I'm sorry," I stammer, "it just popped out."

A timer goes off, saving my skin.

"You know, I could find a use for you in this menu," he says suddenly. "The preparations would be minimal enough for a novice, with relatively uncomplicated flavor profiles."

Is he considering me for an entrée?

"Oh, thank you, but I don't think I'm up to scratch."

"Why not?"

"Isn't it obvious?" *I'm underweight, graceless, and wrapped in cheap plastic.*

"Not to me. I suspect you have great potential. You seem so versatile." His gaze is intense, and I feel a strange pull low down in my body.

"I appreciate the offer," I stammer. "I really do. But I don't believe I'm prepared for the position."

He sets his mouth in a hard line for a moment, then picks me up in his hand. He adjusts my wrapper and helps me back into the Sub-Zero.

"Very well, Miss Hen. Until we meet again."

I feel a strange charge come through his fingertips before he sets me down. Must be static electricity. I believe I'll never live down the "vegetarian" question. But I have a thrilling, dark intuition that those hands aren't done with me.

Plain Vanilla Chicken

The brandy is definitely not a good idea. But it's time to celebrate—here's to flying the coop, to a new life in the big world! I want to shake my tail. Before I know it, there he is, my Mr. Blades. Somehow he always shows up when I'm feeling vulnerable and raw.

He takes me from the fridge and lays me gently on my back on a platter. His fingers are so strong and commanding, and the alcohol is making me cocky.

"Does this mean you're about to make dinner with me?" I blurt.

His expression is hooded. "No, Chicken. First of all, I don't make dinner, I cook . . . hard," he says. "Second, we need to look at some recipes together. Third, you've had too much brandy and you need a rinse."

Recipes? Me, in a recipe? I hear my subconscious squawking a warning from somewhere far across a brandied mist.

Blades holds me under the faucet. The touch of his hands and the flowing water make my tail convulse deliciously. The tension grows unbearable. I feel precarious, as if I were about to fall for him again. A cluck of longing emerges from deep inside me.

Suddenly we can't help ourselves, and his long-fingered hands are all over me. "I want to cook you," he whispers. "Whole." *Oh my.* I'm heating from the inside out.

He reaches over me to open a colossal cabinet full of spice jars. "Tell me, how do you want it? You choose."

"Want it?" I say, gaping. I'm a roaster. What should I want besides a little salt and pepper?

"Yes you know, spices, method. What recipe?"

Now I finally get it. I feel like such an idiot. *He wants to flavor me.*

I try to hide my disappointment. "I've never been seasoned," I mumble despondently. "Or even, um, *prepped.*"

His mouth presses into a hard line and I can feel his shock and exasperation.

"Never?" he whispers.

"Not like this," I confess.

"No one's ever even crisped you?"

"No . . . and I'm not sure I'm ready for the spicy stuff." The sprawling spice cabinet stands wide open like a kinky taunt. I'm practically pink with embarrassment.

My unconscious squawks with indignation. *Why should I be ashamed?* I may be a tipsy chicken, but I'm a free-range organic tipsy chicken with an unexpired sell-by date. I shouldn't need spicy additives.

For the first time he appears to be at a total loss. He drums his fingers on the cutting board. Finally he seems to reach a decision.

"Into the bowl," he commands, ripping a sheet from a packet of foil. "I don't do vanilla. I've never done vanilla. But tonight we're doing vanilla."

roast chicken with brandy-vanilla butter SERVES 4

4 tablespoons unsalted butter, very soft

1 tablespoon brandy

2 teaspoons vanilla extract

1½ teaspoons sugar

1½ teaspoons coarse kosher salt

1 teaspoon freshly ground black pepper

1 (3½- to 4-pound) chicken, patted dry with paper towels

1 Preheat the oven to 400°F. In a medium bowl, whisk together the butter, brandy, vanilla, sugar, ½ teaspoon salt, and ½ teaspoon black pepper until it forms a smooth, supple spread (at first it will seem to curdle, but continue beating until it submits).

2 Season the chicken, including the cavity, with the remaining 1 teaspoon salt and ½ teaspoon pepper.

3 Fill your hand with butter and gently slide your fingers beneath the skin of the breast, slathering butter on the flesh as you go. Work your way down to the thighs. Repeat until you have used all of the butter.

4 Place the chicken on a rack set over a rimmed baking sheet. Roast until the thigh juices run clear when pierced with the tip of a knife and the skin is crisp and golden, about 1 hour and 15 minutes. Let rest for 10 minutes before carving.

Popped-Cherry Pullet

Vanilla's all right once or twice, but we can't keep that up," he says. My subconscious hides her eyes. *He's way out of my league. A man like him could never get excited about chicken.* How could I think I might ever be what he craves? What does a man like him crave?

He fixes me suddenly with a predatory stare. "We're going to remedy this situation right now."

"What situation?" I ask, alarmed.

"Your situation. You're utterly unseasoned. I'm contemplating *haute cuisine* with you, when you've never been paired with anything, it seems." He cocks his head to the side.

Paired? My inner goddess pulls her head from under her wing.

"I'm going to make dinner with you right now. We'll begin with something sweet, soft, and juicy."

Holy shit.

"I thought you didn't make dinner," I say, my heart pounding. "I thought you just cooked, um, hard."

I hear his stomach growl deeply, the effects of which travel all the way to my tail at the base of my cavity—down *there*.

"Don't think I'm getting all hearts and flowers. This is a step in a process. A process that I think will make a superb finish. I hope you'll think so, too."

I cluck low with anticipation.

His stomach growls again. "Chicken, will you please stop clucking? It's very . . . distracting."

He lays me face down and starts to drizzle my back and thighs with oil.

"Are you sure you want to do this?" he says gently.

"Yes," I beg. "Oh, yes."

"I'm going to cook you now, Miss Hen," he mutters as he opens the door of the oven. He slides me into the oven.

Beneath me is a bed of wet, dark, pitted cherries. The dry heat takes me into its sudden embrace, and my juices flow freely over the torn fruit.

I never thought it would feel like this. I never imagined it could be this good. *B'gaaaawk!*

roasted chicken with cherries and herbs   SERVES 4

1 (3½- to 4-pound) chicken, patted dry with paper towels

1¾ teaspoons coarse kosher salt

½ teaspoon freshly ground black pepper

1 small bunch thyme, rosemary, or sage

1 pound pitted sweet cherries

3 tablespoons extra-virgin olive oil

Lemon wedges, for serving

1   Gently rub the naked chicken all over with 1½ teaspoons of the salt and the pepper, paying attention to the bird's cavity and every crevice. Press the herb sprigs all over the flesh, including the cavity. Place in a bowl, cover, and let marinate expectantly in the fridge for at least 1 hour or up to overnight.

2   When the mood is right, preheat the oven to 400°F. Put the cherries in the bottom of a roasting pan and toss with a tablespoon of the olive oil and the remaining ¼ teaspoon salt.

3   Put a rack on top of the cherries and lay the chicken, breast down, on the rack (remove herbs on the outside of the bird before roasting; you can leave the herbs in the cavity where they are). Drizzle the back and thighs of the chicken with a tablespoon of oil. Roast for 40 minutes, then thrust a wooden spoon into the chicken's nether parts and flip the bird so the breasts are up. Stir the cherries. Drizzle the breasts with the remaining tablespoon of oil and continue to roast until the chicken is juicy and golden and completely done, about 40 to 50 minutes longer. Let rest for 10 minutes. Serve with lemon wedges.

Extra-Virgin Breasts

Two blue eyes twinkle in the light of the open Sub-Zero.

It's not Blades, it's some other guy with an easygoing smile and a box of frozen Tater Tots.

"What do you mean? You have a ton of grub in here," he calls behind him. "And I'm starving!"

"It's not grub," I hear Blades scold. "They're my Ingredients. And you can't have them. They're mine, for my work."

The sound of his voice makes me long to see those strong hands, to feel them on my breast. How does he do that?

"Whatevs, bro. I'm not into your fancy stuff anyway. Hey, what about the chicken? We could just throw it under the boiler. Looks tasty."

"No," Blades says, too quickly. "You can take the Christmas ham. Don't touch the chicken."

Before Blades even finishes the sentence, his brother fixes his famished gaze on the rosy ham. He grins and slices off a tender morsel, which seems to please the ham very much. Then he quickly slices off another chunk, plunging it into a jar of mustard before devouring it. The ham glows excitedly, in a way I've rarely seen. I know what that glow means.

Oh, Ham. She's only just met him.

Meanwhile, Blades reaches into the fridge and gently helps me out. I thrill to the unexpected touch of his hands.

"You have far too much potential to be tossed under a broiler, Miss Hen."

Holy crap. Mr. Blades thinks I have potential.

"Extra-virgin," he whispers, making it sound like forbidden nectar. "I'm going to rub you with extra-virgin olive oil, the best I have."

Once again he turns my drumsticks to molten confit with just his voice. It's a mind-blowing skill. He lays me flat on the cutting board and drizzles me slowly with the thick, golden liquid. Suddenly he stills his hands as a loud ping comes from the other side of the kitchen.

It's his brother working the microwave.

"What's in there?"

"That's my side dish for the ham, bro."

"What is it?"

Blades's brother grins mischievously.

"Taters, baby."

roasted bone-in breast with olive oil, lemon, and rosemary SERVES 4

4 bone-in, skin-on chicken breasts (about 3 pounds total), patted dry with paper towels

1 teaspoon coarse kosher salt

¼ teaspoon freshly ground black pepper

1 lemon, thinly sliced

4 small sprigs rosemary, broken into pieces

3 tablespoons extra-virgin olive oil, the best you have

1 Rub the chicken breasts all over with the salt and pepper. Let rest while the oven preheats to 450°F.

2 Lay the lemon slices and rosemary all over the bottom of a roasting pan and place the chicken on top, leaving space in between the breasts so they have room to crisp up. Drizzle generously with the oil.

3 Roast until the breasts are golden and done through and through, 25 to 30 minutes. Serve hot with the pan juices spooned all over the flesh.

LEARNING THE ROPES

Leaving the skin and bones on the breasts makes them cook up crisp-skinned and succulent. But if you prefer the ease of boneless, skinless chicken breasts, substitute those here and roast for 20 to 25 minutes.

Chicken with a Lardon

What kind of stove is this?" I ask.

"It's a Wolf LP dual-fuel with six dual brass burners and an infrared griddle," he says offhandedly.

Wow. Boys and their toys. He flicks a knob and an outsize burner ignites with a roar of flame. A heady aroma wafts from a gleaming skillet he's rested carefully on top of it. Is that bacon?

I've been placed precariously on the countertop while Blades does his *mise en place*. Once again I feel myself teetering on the edge. The edge of desire, the edge of despair—*the edge of the counter.* Crap.

It all happens in a flash. One minute I'm falling, the next I'm in his arms and he's clasping me tightly to his chest. He smells of bacon and imported onions. It's intoxicating.

He stares down at me with a hungry look. I'm so close I can feel the rumbling deep in his taut belly. Slowly he peels me from my wrapper. The plastic comes away, exposing my naked flesh.

Heat me, heat me, I silently implore, but I can't do more than cluck softly.

"What is it about falling poultry?" he mutters. He carries me in his arms to the sink. "I want to rinse you," he says. "Now." A strong, graceful hand cradles me under the cascading tap water while the other caresses me smoothly over the sink. His manicured fingers move in agonizingly slow arcs across my breast and the crease of my thigh. *Holy cow. What is he doing to me?* There's a burning smell, and in my delirium I wonder if I'm already cooked.

A timer goes off and smoke is rising from the Wolf.

"Ignore it," he breathes as he pats my legs dry. "I have a much better use for bacon."

roasted chicken with bacon and sweet paprika SERVES 4

1 orange
1 tablespoon sweet
  paprika
1½ teaspoons coarse
  kosher salt
1 teaspoon freshly ground
  black pepper
1 teaspoon extra-virgin
  olive oil
1 (3½- to 4-pound)
  chicken, patted dry
  with paper towels
4 ounces bacon (about
  4 strips)

1 Preheat the oven to 400°F. Finely grate the zest of the orange into a bowl. Stir in the paprika, salt, and pepper.

2 Massage the oil all over the skin of the chicken. Sprinkle some of the paprika mixture into the cavity; massage the remaining mixture all over the bird (you'll know you've done a good job if your hand begins to redden). Cut the orange into quarters and thrust the fruit deep into the cavity of the bird.

3 Move the chicken to a rack set over a roasting pan. Roast for 45 minutes, basting with any pan juices occasionally. Crisscross the bacon over the breasts. Continue to roast until the chicken is cooked through and the bacon is crisp, about 20 minutes longer. Let rest 10 minutes before carving.

Please Don't Stop Chicken

He sits down at the table, and jeez, does he look hot. He pulls off his white apron and runs a hand through that amazing just-cooked hair. I think I could faint before he even takes a bite.

I'm in warm pieces all over the plate. My own juices mingle with the sticky sweet jam he's spread all over me. My skin feels melting and soft. He ignores the fine silver flatware and picks up a thigh with both hands. *Wow.* He slowly closes his mouth around my thigh, causing clear, hot juice to drip over his delectable lower lip.

"You're so sweet, so succulent, so good," he says in a low voice.

My inner goddess writhes in her velvet coop, licking her own wings and breast as if insatiable. She's making a real meal of herself.

"Yes, oh, yes," I breathe. I want him to finish me, every last bite. I'm his and only his. *Engulf me, devour me, consume me.*

He stills and lays my thigh back down on the plate. He looks troubled.

"Too good," he sighs. He closes his eyes, takes a deep breath, and gives a small shake of his head as if in answer to an invisible waiter.

"Chicken, I'm not the right man for you. You're perfect as you are. My singular tastes would only lead you astray. You should stay well clear of me."

What? Where is this coming from?

"You deserve hearts and flowers, and I can't give you that. I'm sorry. I'm going to set the fork down and let you go now." He gently pushes the plate away.

I'm devastated and heartbroken. He doesn't crave me. *He's really not hungry for me.* Somehow I have royally fouled up dinner.

My inner goddess doesn't seem to notice at first, overcome as she is by her own succulence. Then she looks up from her nibbling to search the emptiness for something to go with it. But there's nothing.

She calls sadly, *Taters, baby?*

baked chicken with apricot jam, sage, and lemon zest SERVES 4

1 (3½- to 4-pound) chicken, cut into 8 pieces, patted dry with paper towels

1¼ teaspoons coarse kosher salt

¾ teaspoon freshly ground black pepper

5 sprigs fresh sage

3 tablespoons extra-virgin olive oil

1 lemon

⅓ cup apricot jam, large chunks cut up

1 teaspoon Worcestershire sauce

1 large garlic clove, minced

1 In a large bowl, gently massage the chicken limbs and breasts with salt and pepper. Add the sage and a tablespoon of the oil and toss well. Let marinate in the fridge until the chicken is begging you for it, about 6 hours or overnight.

2 Preheat the oven 400°F. Grate the zest from the lemon, then squeeze the juice. Add the zest and juice to a small bowl and mix in the jam, Worcestershire sauce, and garlic.

3 Pluck out the sage from the chicken and discard. Rub the sticky jam all over the chicken parts, then lay them down in a 9 x 13-inch baking dish, leaving plenty of breathing room in between each succulent morsel. Bake for 45 to 55 minutes, until the skin is alluringly golden and the juices run clear when pricked. Serve hot and be prepared to burn your fingers.

LEARNING THE ROPES

If your jam tastes lean toward other juicy fruits, feel free to substitute for the apricot. Ginger preserves will spice it up, marmalade will tart it up, and raspberry will make it blush bright red.

Jerked-Around Chicken

The ham is giddy with curiosity when I return to the fridge, but her smile vanishes when she sees that I'm in pieces.

"Oh, no—what's that bastard done to you?"

Crap, not now. Not another grilling from the baked ham.

"Nothing . . . everything's fine," I chirp, but she can always see right through me.

"You've really fallen hard for this guy, haven't you?"

Man, if she only knew. The fact is I see less and less of the ham, as Blade's brother keeps slicing off naughty little bits each night. There's even a bite mark near her rump. She can't repress a goofy, glazed smile.

"If he's an asshole who's just going to burn you, then dump him. But I can tell he likes you by the way he stares at you."

"He has a funny way of showing it."

"Oh, he's into you. But he'd better watch himself," she threatens.

"Please, I'm fine," I lie.

"You need rest," she says warmly. "Put this on. I was going to use it myself, but you need it worse than I do." There's a bowl of marinade next to her.

The ham is an angel. I crawl into the bowl and let myself sink into the liquid. It's bracing and aromatic. It doesn't make me forget my troubles, but somehow it's perfect. I've been seduced by a shifty mystery man, who then dumps me for no obvious reason.

I brood in the luscious marinade. Some jerks are nicer than others.

jerk chicken with spices, rum, chiles, and lime SERVES 4

1 teaspoon whole allspice

4 whole cloves

1 cinnamon stick

1 cup chopped scallions, white and green parts

¼ cup soy sauce

1 lime, zested and juiced

2 Scotch bonnet or serrano chile peppers, seeded and minced

2 tablespoons dark rum

2 tablespoons olive oil

1 tablespoon dried thyme

1 tablespoon light brown sugar

2 teaspoons kosher salt

2 fat garlic cloves, chopped

1 tablespoon grated peeled fresh gingerroot

½ teaspoon freshly grated nutmeg

1 (3½- to 4-pound) chicken, cut into 8 pieces and patted dry with a paper towel

1 In a small dry skillet over medium heat, place the allspice, cloves, and cinnamon. Toast the spices, stirring constantly, until fragrant, 2 to 3 minutes. Transfer the spices to a plate, let cool, then finely grind them in a spice grinder.

2 In a food processor or blender, combine the ground spices, scallions, soy sauce, lime juice and zest, chiles, rum, oil, thyme, brown sugar, salt, garlic, gingerroot, and nutmeg, and process until smooth. Taste and adjust the seasoning if necessary.

3 In a large dish, arrange the chicken in a single layer and pour the marinade over it, tossing to coat. Cover tightly with plastic wrap and marinate in the refrigerator for at least 2 hours, preferably overnight; the longer you delay gratification, the spicier it will be.

4 Preheat the oven to 450°F. Arrange the chicken parts in a single layer on a baking pan lined with foil and heavily oiled. Spoon the excess marinade on top. Bake until the chicken is golden, appetizing, and cooked through, 35 to 45 minutes. Eat while hot, hot, hot.

Spicy Fowl

He's back. Yesterday he sent me some parsley and a *bouquet garni*. I can't keep up with his mood shifts, but I'm a sucker for aromatics.

Today he's going to extra lengths to soften me up. He's got me in a hot soak with more aromatics, plus something mysteriously piquant. It was impossible to stay mad at him when he brought me the beer.

"I just couldn't stop thinking about you," he says. "There's something about you, Miss Hen. I don't know what it is. But I find I must have you."

I am dumbstruck by his hungry expression. Wow . . . to be desired by this great, golden god of a cook.

"Now, if we're going to do this, we need to talk about recipes," he says sharply. *Uh-oh, here it comes.* I steel myself for bad news, and my subconscious does a duck-and-cover.

"First, as my Ingredient, you will submit entirely to my control. I will cook you any time, any way I want—as the mood strikes me."

Jeez. Moods like his could keep a girl hopping.

"What does that mean, your 'Ingredient'?" I ask.

"It means that for the foreseeable future I will cook you, and only you."

He wants to cook me. Blades wants to cook me! And I realize, in a flash of insight, that's exactly what I want. Maybe it's just the beer talking or the way the chiles are making my skin tingle, but right now what I want most in all the world is to satisfy this man's chicken cravings.

"And in return, you will surrender your body to my gastronomic virtuosity. You will be my obedient Ingredient—warm or cold, dressed or undressed, whole or in parts." He pauses to stir my bath. "Or highly spiced."

I'm still on the fence about this. "Why would I want to do such a thing?"

"To please my palate," he breathes, savoring the words.

His voice is hypnotic and the bath has had its effect. I'm soft and pliant, and suddenly I feel prepared for anything he can dish out.

"And lastly, Miss Hen," he adds firmly, "when we're cooking, you will address me as Chef."

"I will consider your proposal . . ." I cluck demurely. "Chef."

chicken chili   SERVES 8

5 tablespoons extra-virgin olive oil

3 pounds ground chicken, preferably a mix of dark and white meat

1 tablespoon coarse kosher salt

1 teaspoon freshly ground black pepper

2 tablespoons tomato paste

2 onions, chopped

1 green bell pepper, seeded and diced

4 garlic cloves, chopped

1 serrano or jalapeño chile peppers, chopped

2 to 3 tablespoons chili powder, to taste

1 (28-ounce) can whole peeled tomatoes

1 bottle dark beer

3 cups cooked pinto beans or 2 (15-ounce) cans, drained and rinsed

½ cup chopped fresh cilantro

2½ tablespoons fresh lime juice, or to taste

Sour cream, for serving

Grated cheddar cheese, for serving

1 Heat 2 tablespoons of the oil in a large pot over medium-high heat. Add half of the chicken and brown it well all over, stirring, 5 to 7 minutes. Season the chicken with ¾ teaspoon salt and ½ teaspoon pepper. Transfer the chicken to a paper towel–lined platter. Repeat with the remaining chicken, 2 tablespoons of oil, another ¾ teaspoon salt, and the pepper.

2 Add the remaining tablespoon of oil to the pan and then stir in the tomato paste. Cook, stirring, until the paste is fragrant, 1 to 2 minutes. Stir in the onions, bell pepper, garlic, and serrano or jalapeño. Cook until the vegetables are golden, about 10 minutes. Stir in the chili powder and remaining 1½ teaspoons salt; cook 1 minute. Return the chicken to the pot. Add the tomatoes, beer, beans, and 1 cup water. Reduce the heat to medium and simmer very gently until thick, about 30 minutes. Stir in the cilantro and the lime juice to taste.

3 Ladle the chili into bowls. Serve topped with sour cream and cheddar cheese.

LEARNING THE ROPES

How spicy do you like your fowl? If you want the pleasure of a seared tongue, leave the seeds in the chiles. If you prefer a milder, slower build to spicy satisfaction, you can de-seed them (use gloves or you'll regret it later). The choice of how to enjoy this is yours.

Learning to Truss You

Trust me?" he whispers.

"Yes . . ." That is not entirely true, and my pulse starts to race.

"Good girl. Do you have any idea what I'm about to do to you?" he asks, caressing my raised breast with a coil of 16-ply twine. The touch of the natural filament is shockingly sensual. The deepest, darkest parts of me clench in the most delicious fashion.

"No," I breathe.

"No, what?" he asks menacingly.

"No, Chef."

He takes a tangerine and eases it slowly, slowly into my orifice until it's buried in me. *Oh, the fullness.*

His deft fingers draw a length of twine from the coil. Adrenaline spikes through me like a carving fork.

He ties my ankles together tightly. The twine is tight but not so that it bites into my skin. I feel restrained but strangely free. An electric charge thrills dangerously up my spine.

"You have a captivating, perfect tail, Miss Hen," he says. "How I will enjoy biting it." *Oh my.*

He inserts me into the Wolf and my flesh succumbs to the rushing waves of heat. Juices flow in torrents inside me as my doneness builds, engorging me down *there*—and everywhere else. I have never felt so ready. So evenly, so dreamily ready.

He pulls me out of the oven.

"Hmm. You are so sweet, Miss Chicken." He reaches over for a package of foil and rips off a sheet.

My body is responding—*now*. All it takes is one quick thrust of the meat thermometer, and I become all flesh and sensation, my gushing juices running utterly clear.

roasted chicken with tangerine and sage   SERVES 4

1 (3½- to 4-pound)
   chicken, patted dry with
   paper towels
1½ teaspoons coarse
   kosher salt
1 teaspoon freshly ground
   black pepper
1 tangerine, cut into
   quarters
1 small bunch sage leaves
Extra-virgin olive oil, for
   drizzling

LEARNING THE ROPES

Much pleasure and satisfaction is to be had from tying up your bird. Not only does it show your chicken who's boss, but a tight binding ensures the chicken cooks exactly how you want it—evenly, moist, and tender. It also closes off the chicken's cavity, so the juices swelling within can't spill out, at least not until you're ready for them.

1   Preheat the oven to 400°F. Season the chicken all over, including the cavity, with the salt and pepper. Thrust the tangerine and sage deep into the cavity of the chicken.

2   Move the stuffed bird, breast side up, splayed legs facing you, on a large, empty surface where you will have plenty of space for maneuvering. Take a 30-inch length of butcher's twine and string it underneath the chicken's back. Pull both sides of the string up over the chicken's wings. Cross the ends of the strings over each other and give them a yank, pulling the wings tight to the body (see photo 1, page 36). Do not slacken or let go of the twine.

3   Now that you have tightly secured the wings, it is time to bind the body and legs. Pull the ends of the twine underneath the legs, crossing it underneath the bird, and wrap it around the ankles, binding them together. Wrap twine several times to make sure the ankles are tightly bound (see photo 2, page 37). Wrap the twine around the tail, pulling it tight to close up the cavity. Give the twine once last tug to make sure the bindings are secure, then knot the string. Trim any excess twine and step back to admire your handiwork.

4   Place the chicken breast side up on a rack set over a rimmed baking sheet. Drizzle with oil. Roast until the thigh juices run clear when pierced with the tip of a knife and the skin is crisp and golden, about 1 hour and 15 minutes. Let rest 20 minutes before cutting the restraints and having your way with it.

Holy Mole Chicken

He picks me up from the shelf and I notice for the first time an ingredients list posted on the door of the Sub-Zero. His list reads as bossy and kinky as he talks, and it includes peanuts, chocolate, raisins—*and me*. Pervy.

"Are we making cookies?" I cluck coquettishly.

He glances at the list and narrows his eyes at me playfully. "No, Miss Hen. I haven't figured out how to make you a dessert. Yet." He quirks his lips into a smile. "I have something more—elaborate—planned for today."

"Ah, well. What if I don't feel elaborate today?"

"You don't want to cook?" he asks.

"Not *just* cook," I murmur tentatively. Am I really going to ask?

"I see." He frowns.

Okay, here goes nothing.

"I want you to make dinner with me. Simple. Normal. Unfinessed."

His face clouds. Shit, this isn't going well.

He cocks his head from one side to the other. And again. Jeez, he's really discombobulated.

"You want candles and linen, hearts and flowers," he says. "But I don't know how to do that, Chicken. My tastes are very particular."

"I want you to taste only me. Taste me for what I am. Clean your plate. Mop up my juices with bread . . ."

He takes a dazed step back, and for a moment the air grows tense.

"Please," I whisper.

"I don't know," he mutters, and he stalks off to find something.

My subconscious is hopping mad. *Now you've done it. You've made him chicken out.*

But he returns with that foxy look in his eyes. His apron hangs off his hips in that way that makes my whole body gabble with glee. He's holding something. It's a chunk of chocolate.

Oh shit, he really knows how to distract a girl.

I still wish he'd make dinner with me, with me tasting like me. But maybe it's okay to let him cook me if there's chocolate involved. Just this once.

roasted chicken legs with mole sauce

SERVES 4 TO 6

---

2 teaspoons coarse kosher salt

3 chicken legs, thighs and drumsticks separated (about 3 pounds total)

1 tablespoon coriander seeds

½ teaspoon whole black peppercorns

2 whole cloves

2 chipotle chiles in adobo sauce, seeded if you like it soft and mild

2 plum tomatoes, roughly chopped

1 small white onion, roughly chopped

¼ cup roasted, salted peanuts, plus chopped peanuts for garnish (optional)

¼ cup raisins

3 ounces bittersweet chocolate, grated or chopped

3 garlic cloves, chopped

2 teaspoons dried oregano

1 teaspoon ground cinnamon

2 tablespoons extra-virgin olive oil, plus more as needed

Lime wedges, for serving

Cooked rice, for serving

1 Massage 1¼ teaspoons of salt all over the chicken legs.

2 To make the mole, warm a small skillet over medium-high heat. Add the coriander seeds, black peppercorns, and cloves and toast the spices until they are fragrant and start to smoke, 2 to 3 minutes. Transfer the spices to a blender and add ½ cup water, the chipotle chilies, tomatoes, onion, peanuts, raisins, chocolate, garlic, oregano, cinnamon, and remaining ¾ teaspoon salt and blend until smooth.

3 Center a rack in the oven and preheat to 325°F.

4 In a Dutch oven over high heat, warm the olive oil. Add the chicken legs in batches and sear until golden brown and crisp on all sides, about 8 minutes, adding more oil to the pan if needed. Pour the mole over the waiting legs, making sure it coats the meat evenly, cover the pan, and bring to a simmer over high heat. Transfer to the oven and bake until the meat is very tender, about 1 hour, turning the legs after 30 minutes.

5 If the sauce isn't as thick and glossy as you want it, transfer the chicken legs to a serving platter and cover with foil to keep warm. Put the pot back on the stove and bring the liquid to a simmer. Let the sauce reduce and thicken until it's exactly how you like it. Skim off any fat before serving. Garnish with chopped peanuts if they turn you on, and lime wedges. Enjoy this on a soft bed of fluffy rice.

Hot Rubbed Hen

You really can't keep buying me things." I'm looking furiously at yet another spice he's purchased.

"I like you in fine things," he replies. "I have the means. Besides, there's a recipe—"

"To hell with the recipes!" I interrupt, fuming. I can't keep up with him. Every night it's some hot new preparation. And this one looks downright fiery.

"But the harissa will be good on you. It will test your limits. And mine." He smiles that searing smile, and my bones loosen. Involuntarily I relent.

He goes to the stereo to put on some loud pop music. He coats a brush with the hot paste. He lashes the harissa into my skin with the brush. *Ow*—it smarts. But quickly my skin is singing at its touch. He strokes my neck and shoulders, painting a trail of fire leading all the way down there. *Hot damn.*

He slips two fingers inside me, making me gasp. The touch of his spiced fingertips ignites hot sparks under my skin that fire into my bloodstream and pulse around my body, heating everything in their path. I groan . . . Oh my—a conflagration radiates throughout my cavity . . . everywhere. *Fuck.*

I'm building unstoppably. He continues to paint my skin with fire, in slow, even strokes at first . . . but as his control unravels, the brush moves faster and faster. My back arches as I open myself to the consuming, punishing, heavenly sensation . . . pushing me, pushing me . . . Scoville unit after Scoville unit . . . spiraling into a peppery paroxysm. When I think I can take no more, he abruptly stills.

His breathing ragged, he turns me gently over onto a soft bed of beans.

"You wear that well," he says. "Keep it on for the rest of the day. I'll cook you tonight."

roasted chicken with harissa, preserved lemons, chickpeas, and mint SERVES 4

1½ cups cooked chickpeas, rinsed if from a can (use one 15-ounce can)

1 large red onion, peeled and cut into ½-inch chunks

2 garlic cloves, thinly sliced

5 tablespoons plus 1 teaspoon extra-virgin olive oil

2 teaspoons harissa or other hot sauce

2 tablespoons seeded and chopped preserved lemon

2 teaspoons coarse kosher salt

½ teaspoon freshly ground black pepper

1 teaspoon dried thyme

½ teaspoon ground allspice

1 (3½- to 4-pound) chicken, patted dry with paper towels

Mint leaves, for serving

1 In a medium bowl, stir the chickpeas, onion, and garlic with 3 tablespoons of the olive oil and 1 teaspoon of the harissa; scatter on the bottom of a roasting pan.

2 In a small bowl, mix together the preserved lemon, salt, pepper, thyme, and allspice. Massage it all over the chicken flesh, especially inside of the cavity. In a small bowl, whisk the remaining harissa with a teaspoon oil. Use a brush to coat the skin with the harissa mixture.

3 Lay the chicken on top of the beans, breast side down. Cover the chicken with foil or plastic wrap and let sit in the refrigerator for at least 30 minutes and up to 1 day.

4 Let the chicken warm up at room temperature while the oven preheats to 375°F.

5 Roast the chicken for 20 minutes, then thrust a wooden spoon into the cavity of the bird and flip so the breast side is up. Continue to cook until the chicken is golden brown and cooked through, about 25 to 30 minutes longer. Serve with mint leaves.

LEARNING THE ROPES

Harissa is an intense chile sauce from Northern Africa. It's spicy, searing hot. If you can't find it, substitute the hottest hot sauce you can get.

Mustard-Spanked Chicken

Oh, Chicken, did you just cluck at me?"

Crap.

"No," I squawk hoarsely.

"I believe you did. Yes, you did. You remember what I said I'd do to you if you clucked?"

Aw, jeez. "Yes." I pause before I add, "Yes, Chef."

"My word is my bond," he crows. "I'm going to spank you. And then I will cook you, very hot and hard."

I know what his hard cooking is like.

"I'm not sure I can take any more quite yet," I whine.

"Stamina, Miss Hen," he says brightly.

My inner goddess has donned a tiny cheerleader's uniform and starts to chant.

Give me a B!

Whack.

Give me an L! Give me an A!

Whack whack.

Give me a D! E! S!

Whack whack whack.

What does that spell?

Control-freak poultry-beater, that's what it spells. But I don't fancy another swat, so I manage to keep the thought to myself for once.

He roasts me gently until I reach sweet doneness.

"You are a most beautiful sight," he says, pulling me out of the Wolf. "And your smell is intoxicating."

Afterward, everywhere he spanked me is stinging and warm. The experience was humiliating and mustardy and unbelievably hot. I definitely don't want him to do that to me again. But now that it's over I have this warm, safe, golden brown afterglow. I feel contented, and totally confused.

I must remember to cluck at him more often.

roasted chicken with mustard, fresh basil, and garlic SERVES 4

1 (3½- to 4-pound) chicken, patted dry with paper towels

1 teaspoon coarse kosher salt, plus more to taste

½ teaspoon freshly ground black pepper

2 tablespoons Dijon mustard

2 teaspoons minced fresh basil

2 garlic cloves, minced

3 tablespoons extra-virgin olive oil

1 Rub the chicken all over, including the cavity, with the salt and pepper.

2 In a small bowl, stir together the mustard, basil, and garlic and slap it hard onto the bird everywhere you just rubbed the salt and pepper. Refrigerate overnight or for at least 1 hour so it can recover.

3 Preheat the oven to 400°F. Place a rack in a roasting pan.

4 Carefully lay the bird on the rack, breast side down. Drizzle with 1 tablespoon of the oil. Roast for 30 minutes. Thrust a wooden spoon into the chicken cavity and flip the bird over so the breasts are up; drizzle with the remaining oil. Continue to roast until the bird is golden brown and quite done, about 30 to 40 minutes longer. Enjoy.

LEARNING THE ROPES

If you've got a fridge full of epicurean mustards at the ready (brandy, cognac, horseradish, honey, green peppercorn, etc.), feel free to substitute for the Dijon. Treat your bird right and she'll reward you crisply.

Totally Fried Chicken

Fry?" *We're going to fry?*

"Yes, and fast. The Wolf does 16,000 BTUs in a single burner."

Suddenly a thousand butterflies are moshing in my belly. *Holy shit, what kind of caper is he planning this time?* I'm not sure I'm prepared for this.

"I'll prepare you, darling. Don't worry," he says dryly. He must be telepathic. It's uncanny.

But am I a fryer? Maybe I come across that way, but I've always thought of myself as more of a roaster, a low-heat bird. No way do I have legs plump enough for batter and hot oil.

"Do you like to fry?" I ask a little timidly.

"It requires intense preparation and control. How could I not?"

He flicks on the Wolf with a roar and sets a heavy Dutch oven on top. It's a beast of a pot—big, solid, enameled flame-red. He pops in a thermometer, and its bright red tongue shoots up in sync with my soaring desire. *Oh, I'm prepped, all right.*

Blades is already sifting flour. His hands expertly shake a perfect bed of powder onto the plate. He's just so competent.

"On the plate," he commands, and rolls me around in the flour like a pro.

Hot damn. I'm nearly cooked from just the heat of his fingertips. My inner goddess is swooning in her red velvet coop. She crows with ecstasy when, with a sudden shake, he de-flours me.

With a loud whoosh of oil I'm frying. I'm really frying. Is there anything this aproned Adonis can't do? I have a vision of myself as Icarus, wings singeing as he nears the sun.

But my wings aren't burned—they're flaky and crisp and *delicious*.

crispy fried chicken SERVES 4 TO 6

1½ teaspoons coarse
   kosher salt
½ teaspoon cayenne
   pepper
½ teaspoon freshly
   ground black pepper
1 (3½- to 4-pound)
   chicken, cut into
   10 pieces and patted
   dry with paper towels
Peanut oil, lard, or chicken
   fat, for frying
2 eggs
¼ cup buttermilk
1½ cups all-purpose flour
¼ teaspoon baking
   powder

1 Rub the salt, cayenne pepper, and black pepper all over
   the chicken parts and let sit in the refrigerator for as
   long as possible, from 20 minutes to 24 hours.

2 Fill a large Dutch oven with 3 inches of fat and heat it to
   375°F. In a medium bowl, whisk together the eggs with
   the buttermilk. Whisk together the flour and baking
   powder and place in a shallow dish.

3 Dip the chicken pieces first into the egg and buttermilk
   mixture and then into the flour mixture, shaking off
   any excess. Add 4 pieces of the chicken to the pan
   and fry, covered, for 6 minutes. Uncover, turn the
   chicken, and continue to cook until golden brown and
   crisp on the outside and just cooked through, about 7
   minutes longer for dark meat and 5 minutes for white
   meat. Drain on a rack before serving. Repeat with the
   remaining chicken pieces.

Cream-Slicked Chick

Y ou have the most beautiful skin, pale and not one feather. I want to crisp every single inch of it."

"You can crisp me any time," I purr.

"How about a little honey and spice?" he asks suggestively.

I can't help but cluck derisively. His spice thing is out of control. I know I'm pushing it, as my inner goddess pokes her head out of her golden henhouse.

"You didn't just cluck, did you?"

"Oh no," I answer quickly.

"I'm going to drizzle this on you," he says.

"You really know how to warm a chick up." I pause before adding, "Chef."

His eyes flash with irritation. "You have a smart mouth, for someone without a head," he whispers. "I may have to do something about that."

My inner goddess high-fives me with a feathered wing. *I've gotten under his skin.* Holy crap.

crisp baked chicken with honey mustard and lime   SERVES 4

2 tablespoons cream

2 tablespoons honey mustard

1 garlic clove, minced

1 lime, zested and juiced

½ teaspoon freshly ground black pepper

1 (3½- to 4-pound) chicken, cut into 8 pieces, patted dry with paper towels

1 teaspoon coarse kosher salt

Chopped chives

1   Preheat the oven to 400°F. Whisk together the cream, mustard, garlic, lime zest and juice, and pepper. Rub the chicken parts with the salt. Drizzle the cream mixture over the chicken, tossing to coat.

2   Line a jelly-roll pan or baking sheet with a nonstick liner, or with aluminum foil, oiling the foil. Arrange the chicken to fit in a single layer, leaving breathing room between the pieces. Roast for 20 minutes, then raise the oven temperature to 500°F and continue to roast until the chicken is cooked through and golden skinned; the tender breasts will take about 25 minutes, and muscled legs will need 5 to 10 minutes more. Serve the chicken garnished with chives.

Chile-Lashed Fricassee

The ingredients list on the Sub-Zero is unusually detailed today. It's classic Blades—bossy, elaborate, and demanding, and it ends with "PURE New Mexico chile powder."

Jeez. To his usual arsenal of barked commands, bullying stares, and aggressive flavoring, he's now added shouty capitals. Is he trying to impress me or intimidate me? He's so mysterious.

When he struts back into the kitchen, barefoot in jeans and a tight black T-shirt, he places a bag of bright red powder on the counter in front of me.

"I brought us something new to play with today."

I think I'm scared of whatever it is.

But I can't take my mind off the chile. It looks dangerous, exotic, hot. I imagine his skilled fingers rubbing that tangy sting deep into my skin. *Who's hot tonight,* squawks my inner goddess, *who's hot tonight?* She's got a little pitchfork and she's thrusting it up and down suggestively. I'm really not sure what she's trying to tell me with that one, but somehow it's convincing.

He's at the front burner of the Wolf sweating onions and peppers, his apron hanging off his hips in that special way. He pours himself a little wine and sways to music only he can hear. I feel loose-limbed, my bones like jelly.

My stars. The onions aren't the only thing he's sweating.

chicken fricassee with prosciutto, tomatoes, and sweet peppers SERVES 4

1 (3½- to 4-pound) chicken, cut into 8 pieces, patted dry with paper towels

2 teaspoons coarse kosher salt, plus more to taste

½ teaspoon freshly ground black pepper

1 cup dry white wine

6 garlic cloves, thinly sliced

1 teaspoon pure chile powder such as New Mexico

1 teaspoon sweet paprika

½ teaspoon crushed red pepper flakes

2 tablespoons extra-virgin olive oil, more as needed

2 ounces chopped prosciutto or other cured ham

2 small red onions, each cut into 6 wedges

2 red bell peppers, cut into ½-inch-thick strips

6 plum tomatoes (1½ pounds), halved lengthwise or quartered if large

1 cup unsalted chicken broth or water

Fresh basil, for serving

1 Rub the chicken with the salt and pepper, and let it rest in a baking pan. Mix together the wine, garlic, chile powder, paprika, and red pepper flakes and pour over the chicken. Cover with plastic wrap and marinate overnight in the refrigerator, turning the chicken once.

2 Preheat the oven to 325°F.

3 Remove the chicken from the marinade, reserving the marinade. Pat the chicken dry. Heat a Dutch oven or very large cast-iron skillet over medium-high heat and warm 1 tablespoon of the olive oil. Add the prosciutto and sear on all sides until golden brown around the edges, 1 to 2 minutes. Using a slotted spoon, transfer the prosciutto to a plate and set aside. Add another tablespoon of olive oil to the pan. Add the chicken and sear in batches on all sides over medium-high heat until golden brown, 8 to 10 minutes (add more oil if necessary). Transfer the chicken as it browns to a plate.

4 Add the onions and bell peppers to the pan and cook over medium heat until tender, 7 to 10 minutes. Add the reserved marinade and, over high heat, reduce the liquid by half. Return chicken and prosciutto to the pan and add the tomatoes and broth. Cover and bake until the chicken is tender, 50 minutes to an hour, uncovering the pan after 30 minutes. If the sauce is thin, transfer chicken and vegetables to a platter and tent with foil. Bring sauce to a simmer on the stove. Reduce until thickened (this could take 20 to 30 minutes). Season with more salt if needed. Pour over the chicken and garnish with basil.

Pulled Pullet

Have you ever wondered what's on the other side of your limits?" he asks. Without waiting for an answer he punches something into the stereo remote. *Holy fuck, what's he going to do next?*

A stormy surge of strings issues from unseen speakers, while Blades pinches gently at my flesh. It's just a little tickle at first, but as the music builds, so does he. Suddenly, sharply, he pulls a strand of dark meat from my drumstick.

"B'gawk!" I cry out. It takes me by surprise, but I find I like how it feels. It tingles. He does it again, harder.

As the music surges on, his fingers dig more deeply into my flesh, stripping morsel after morsel of my body in perfect time with the music. It's a sweet agony, as he strips me down with his masterful fingers. I am drawn deeper into my most hidden desires by the delicious sensation and the otherworldly harmony of strings and winds.

The music stills a moment and so does he. Then a second musical theme emerges, less stormy than the first—in my mind I see the motions of a hen as she crosses a country road. Something dangerous and irresistible pulls her toward the storm on the other side. The birdlike warble of a single oboe floats over the strutting strings, as Blades's deft fingers continue to ravish my pulchritude . . . pluck and pluck again . . . but the music, transporting me . . . his fingers deconstructing me . . . *Yes, I get this.* I've navigated into a dark and carnal place. When at last the music drives for its climax, so do I, churning and flying apart like a blender on liquefy. *Wow.*

"What was that music?" I groan incomprehensibly as I recover.

"The allegro from 'The Hen'—Joseph Haydn's Symphony No. 83 in G Minor," he says. He inserts me between two soft buns. "For some reason I've always wanted to cook to it."

The vision of the country hen comes to me again. It's so mysterious. But I think I know now why she crossed the road.

barbecued chicken sandwiches   SERVES 6

FOR THE BARBECUE SAUCE

2 tablespoons extra-virgin
   olive oil

1 large onion, chopped

3 garlic cloves, minced

¾ cup light molasses

⅔ cup white wine vinegar

3 tablespoons tomato
   paste

1 teaspoon coarse kosher
   salt

1 teaspoon Tabasco or
   other chile sauce, plus
   more for serving

½ teaspoon dry mustard
   powder

½ teaspoon ground
   coriander

½ teaspoon freshly
   ground black pepper

1 fully cooked rotisserie
   chicken

6 soft buns, toasted and
   buttered, for serving

1 sweet onion, thinly sliced
   (optional)

Shredded cabbage or
   lettuce, for serving
   (optional)

Pickles, for serving
   (optional)

1 To prepare the barbecue sauce, in a large saucepan
   over medium-high heat, warm the oil. Add the onion
   and garlic and cook, stirring, until the onions are soft
   and browned, about 15 minutes. Transfer the mixture
   to the bowl of a food processor or blender. Add the
   molasses, vinegar, tomato paste, salt, Tabasco sauce,
   and spices and puree until smooth. Return the mixture
   to the saucepan and cook over medium-low heat,
   stirring occasionally, until the sauce has thickened
   slightly, about 15 minutes.

2 Gently pull apart the chicken, taking care to gather
   every bit of flesh, wresting it from the bone; chop any
   large pieces of skin into bite-size morsels. Toss the
   chicken bits with just enough of the barbecue sauce
   to coat it. Taste and stir in more of the hot sauce if you
   want it even hotter.

3 Stuff the pulled pullet into the hot, buttered buns and
   top with onion, cabbage, and pickles, if using. Enjoy.

Basted Bird

I'm dripping and fragrant as he helps me out of the basin—white stoneware, egg-shaped, and very stylish. A scent of thyme and expensive oil clings to my skin as he sets me on a clean white kitchen towel. I consider how I must look. I still can't believe this prince of the kitchen wants a pale, underweight ugly duckling like me. Surely there's been some mistake.

"Hey," he says, jolting me back to the present. "You're a gorgeous, perfect bird, a beautiful swan of a chicken. Don't droop your neck like that." He tilts me up to let the last of the marinade flow out of me. His eyes are soft and warm. He quirks his mouth into a smile. "Trust me?" he asks in a low voice.

"Yes," I breathe, unsure but unable to say anything more. Deep longing oozes in the marrow of my bones.

"Good," he says. "I have plans for you." He's holding something in his hand, but I can't quite make it out.

He turns me away from him, leaving my backside totally at his mercy. Slowly and gently, he pushes something deep inside me. It's a lemon from the marinade. It fills me deliciously, as he simultaneously slips two long, knowing fingers within me. They trace slow circles reaching nearly all the way inside, and then back to the opening. *Holy fuck*, his fingers are so deep inside me. Those stunning hands are caressing my most secret parts, seasoning me to the point of eruption.

My inner goddess is running fast from side to side of her chicken run, as if she has lost her head.

The Wolf is already preheated and waiting—as always, he's planned ahead. He places me on my back in a shallow bath of water. I feel a wet heat suffuse me, penetrating everywhere inside and out. I am melty and delectable.

It's not long before I feel my doneness build, and when it comes it's one of the most intense yet. My inner goddess bolts madly across her run.

The sky is falling, the sky is falling!

roasted chicken with carrots, celery, and onion SERVES 4 TO 6

1 (4½- to 5-pound) chicken, patted dry with paper towels

½ cup extra-virgin olive oil

1 lemon, thinly sliced

1 small bunch of fresh thyme

2 teaspoons coarse kosher salt

1 teaspoon freshly ground black pepper

3 medium carrots, peeled and halved lengthwise, then cut crosswise into quarters

2 celery stalks, cut crosswise into thirds

1 large onion, peeled and cut into 1½-inch chunks

1 Cradle the chicken in a large bowl. Add the oil, lemon, thyme, salt, and pepper; toss well, making sure to caress the inside of the cavity, coating it with seasonings. Cover tightly and transfer to the refrigerator to rest overnight.

2 The next day, let the chicken warm up at room temperature for 30 minutes while you preheat the oven to 450°F. Remove the lemon slices and thyme from the marinade and press them deep inside the chicken's cavity. Scatter the vegetables over the bottom of a roasting pan. Pour just enough water into the pan to moisten the bottom. Arrange the chicken, breast side up, on top of the bed of vegetables.

3 Transfer the pan to the center oven rack; roast for 20 minutes. Baste the juices all over the bird, and continue roasting, basting every 10 to 15 minutes for 35 minutes more (if the chicken is not golden brown all over at this point, continue to cook for 10 more minutes). Reduce the heat to 325°F. Finish roasting, without basting, until the chicken is cooked through and the thigh juices run clear, 20 to 35 minutes longer. Let the chicken stand for 5 minutes before carving. Serve with the pan juices and vegetables, if desired.

Cock au Vin

The lists are getting more frequent and more overbearing. He plies me with aromatics, rubs me with oil, flecks me with spice. My vitals clench deliciously as I recall his deft hands, the slow, low heat, even his fussy way of making dinner.

My unconscious clucks at me. *Not making dinner. Cooking,* she cackles. I ignore her as best I can, but she's awfully shrill.

She has a point. I know he needs more than just white and dark meat with a bit of crispy skin. He craves spice, not sustenance. And I crave him.

I'm distracted from my musings by the pop of a cork. Blades is opening a bottle of fine red wine. He's wearing his usual white apron that hangs, in that way, off his hips. *Holy cats.*

"Burgundy okay with you?"

"You know I know nothing about wine. I'm sure it's great." My voice cracks as I speak. There's already a heady smell of bacon wafting from the gleaming cooktop. It's discombobulating. He's planning something special, but what?

There's a loud hiss as he pours some of the wine into the hot pan. He fondles my drumstick with his strong fingers.

"You are mine," he says softly. "Mine alone. Never forget it."

I prevent myself from clucking, but merely make a low sound of assent. Though I might resist the thought, I am his.

"But tonight—I'm having a dinner party."

Holy fuck.

"And I—?"

"Why, you're the main course, Miss Hen."

LEARNING THE ROPES

If your chicken deserves a reward for especially pliant behavior, consider replacing the commonplace creminis with something more enticing. A mix of exotic mushrooms—oyster, chanterelle, shiitake—gives the sauce a richer flavor.

braised chicken with red wine, mushrooms, and onions SERVES 4 TO 6

4 ounces bacon (about 4 strips)

20 pearl onions, peeled, or 1 large white onion, sliced

1 (3½- to 4- pound) chicken, cut into 8 pieces and patted dry with paper towels

1¼ teaspoons coarse kosher salt

½ teaspoon freshly ground black pepper

Olive oil, if needed

6 garlic cloves, smashed and peeled

2 cups unsalted or low-sodium chicken broth

2 cups red wine

2 bay leaves

4 fresh thyme sprigs

6 fresh parsley sprigs

10 ounces cremini or white button mushrooms, roughly chopped

2 tablespoons unsalted butter, softened

2 tablespoons all-purpose flour

Chopped fresh parsley, for garnish

Egg noodles, for serving

1 In a Dutch oven, brown the bacon. Transfer to a paper towel–lined plate, keeping the fat in the pan. Crumble the bacon.

2 Add half the onions, half the chicken, skin side down, and half the salt and pepper to the pan. Brown the chicken on all sides, about 10 minutes. Transfer to a plate, and repeat with remaining onions, chicken, and salt and pepper, adding a little olive oil to the pan if needed.

3 Add the garlic to the pan and sauté until golden, 2 minutes. Spoon off any excess fat. Add the chicken broth, wine, and herbs. Return the bacon and chicken to the pan. Lower the heat to a simmer. Cover and cook for 20 to 25 minutes, until the chicken is cooked through. The white meat will cook faster than the dark. As each chicken part finishes, transfer it, along with the onions and garlic, to a clean platter. Discard the bay leaves and herb sprigs.

4 Add the mushrooms to the pan and turn the heat to high. Bring to a boil and reduce the liquid by three-fourths, about 15 minutes. Meanwhile, in a small bowl, mix the butter and flour. Lower the heat and whisk in the butter mixture. Simmer until the sauce is thick, 2 to 5 minutes longer. Return the chicken and onions to the pan to reheat. Garnish with parsley and serve on a bed of egg noodles.

two

Falling
to Pieces

Chicken Parts and Bits

B efore you can agree to be my Ingredient, you'll need to understand the recipes."

Recipes? "Do you really need those?" I cluck coquettishly. "I thought we might just wing it."

"No, Miss Hen," he says as if I were an errant chick. "I've told you, I don't just make dinner. What I do requires intricate steps, precise preparations, and careful plating. I hope you'll want to do it too."

He drags out a large cookbook. He opens it to some elaborate recipes, illustrated with shocking and explicit photos of ingredients, raw and cooked, in all kinds of appalling positions. This goes way beyond trussing. I'm simply speechless. Is this what he does—he tortures food?

"You're a sadist?"

"I'm a Foodie." His eyes burn with dark craving.

"What does that mean?" I ask.

"It means I want you to willingly surrender yourself to my recipes. This is what it means to truly be my Ingredient. I want to manipulate your texture, layer your flavors, Chicken. I see you as a foam, a fricassee, a gelée . . . a modern craft cocktail . . ."

I don't understand any of this. *Cock tail?* I think I'm in shock.

"I want to finesse you, very much."

His words from our first meeting come back to me. *It's all about finesse.* I look around the kitchen. Suddenly the knife rack and the spice cabinet seem way more sketchy than before.

"Were there others?"

He closes his eyes. "Yes. But not like you. You've proven yourself both resilient and versatile. Which is why I think that each part of you can be cooked separately to get the doneness right, to make flavors penetrate deeper. In the end, roasting you whole leaves your breast a little less moist than if I cook it separately. These recipes will show us the way."

Separately? *He means cut apart.* It's not just about taking me whole;

now he wants to flavor me limb by limb. Am I ready for more of that? My subconscious picks up the phone to call a taxi.

"I can't keep up . . . why are you like this?" I say.

"Ah, that's a long story. When I was still just a boy someone showed me what cooking could be. Like they do it in Europe. She showed me that cooking wasn't just warming something up. It's the discipline of turning raw ingredients into transcendence. She was the turning point for me."

"She? She who?"

"It doesn't matter, baby. I had a tough introduction to food. As a child I ate nothing but TV dinners and ramen. I was inexperienced. And that's when an older woman took me under her wing and introduced me to the lifestyle."

I am devastated at this image of little Shifty, just a child. And I'm appalled that Mrs. Child-temptress, Mrs. Child-warper, this—this evil old Mrs. Child-whatever figure was allowed to fuck him up so badly. It's because of Mrs. Child he's unable to just make dinner like everyone else. A boy who knew only Salisbury steak and Tater Tots, then some herb-crazed tart shows up with a chicken *chasseur* and has her way with him. The thought depresses me.

"Is that the reason for your shifty moods?" I ask quietly.

"Oh, Chicken, I'm fucked up and shifty as hell. But I'm hungry for you."

Hungry for me! *My Shifty Blades hungers for me.*

Flattered Breasts

How many were there?"

"What?"

"How many Ingredients were there, before me?"

"Do you really want to rehash that conversation again?" He's becoming ruffled.

"Yes! I think I have a right to know."

"Fifteen."

I wasn't expecting that. Fifteen? *Holy shit.* He's really been around. He's so secretive. I feel anger bubbling up inside me.

I glare at him and he glares back. Despite the anger, I feel it, the attraction —irresistible, drawing us together like kitchen magnets.

My breast arches involuntarily toward his touch. Suddenly he seizes me and lays me out on the counter, claiming me hungrily. His fingers pull me taut, the palms of his hands grinding my soft white meat into the hard granite, trapping me. I feel him. His stomach growls, and my mind spins as I acknowledge his craving for me.

"Why must you always challenge me?" he murmurs breathlessly.

"Because I can." My pulse throbs painfully.

He grabs a fistful of kosher salt.

"I'm going to season you now."

"Yes." My voice is low and heated.

He reaches for a rolling pin, then hesitates, looking at me.

"Yes, please, Chef," I moan.

The first blow of the rolling pin jolts me but leaves behind a delicious warm feeling.

"I. Will. Make. You. Mine," he says between blows.

Adrenaline is pounding thunderously through me—and so is he.

Fighting is rough, but making up could be the end of me.

sautéed chicken breasts with garlic, olives, and wine   SERVES 4 TO 6

4 boneless, skinless chicken breast halves (2 pounds), patted dry with paper towels

1½ teaspoons coarse kosher salt

½ teaspoon freshly ground black pepper

3 tablespoons all-purpose flour

2 tablespoons extra-virgin olive oil

3 garlic cloves, minced

Large pinch of crushed red pepper flakes

¼ cup dry white wine

¼ cup low-sodium chicken broth

1 tablespoon freshly squeezed lemon juice

2 tablespoons chopped fresh flat-leaf parsley

2 tablespoons cold unsalted butter, cut into small pieces

2 tablespoons sliced, pitted kalamata olives

Crusty bread, for serving

1 Using the side of a rolling pin, gently slap the breasts into submission, until they are ¼ inch thick. Season with salt and pepper, then sprinkle them on both sides with the flour, knocking off any excess.

2 Heat the oil in a large skillet over medium-high heat. Add the chicken in batches and cook until golden at the edges, 3 to 4 minutes on each side. Transfer the chicken as it cooks to a plate and tent with foil.

3 In the same pan, sauté the garlic and red pepper flakes for about 30 seconds or until fragrant. Add the wine, broth, and lemon juice to the pan, and let simmer, scraping up any browned bits, until the sauce thickens down to a glaze. Add the parsley, butter, and olives, stirring constantly. Taste and add more salt if it needs it. Return the chicken to the pan and cook until heated through, about 2 minutes. Serve hot with crusty bread.

Holy Hell Wings

Blades is standing in front of me dressed in nothing but a white apron and a chef's toque. He has a sticky glob of honey dripping from his long fingers. I lean out to see it better, but invisible chicken wire prevents me. My eyes cross. He moves a little closer and I can smell the glob. There's something strange and powerful about it.

"Now cluck," he commands, his voice soft. My beak opens to obey, but my wattle quivers uncontrollably.

"Enough," he snaps.

I long to taste the honey, to peck at it. I can smell it's not just honey, it has a hot, citrus aroma. Sharp and sweet at the same time. I crane a little farther and the chicken wire is gone, I'm free. I open my wings and he covers them with the sticky hot mess. The spice penetrates me and I feel the familiar pull deep in my belly.

"You're marinating just for me," he says darkly, "all for me."

Yes, I moan. *Let me feed you, only you.* Just then I notice that he's holding something—a radish, I think. The radish starts to pulse like a heart. The image starts to fade, and I start to panic.

"Wake up, baby," he says, opening the Sub-Zero with a triumphant flourish as I come back to reality. "Time for the broiler."

Holy hell.

jalapeño chicken wings with avocado

SERVES 6 TO 8

---

3 pounds chicken wings, patted dry with paper towels

¼ cup olive oil

2 tablespoons hot sauce, plus more for serving

2 tablespoons honey

2 teaspoons tomato paste

4 garlic cloves, chopped

2 jalapeño peppers, roughly chopped (leave in the seeds to make these holy hell hot)

1 lime, zested and juiced

1 teaspoon coarse kosher salt, plus more to taste

2 avocados, peeled, pitted, and sliced

1   The night before feasting, lay the chicken wings in a bowl. Combine the oil, hot sauce, honey, tomato paste, garlic, jalapeño, zest and lime juice, and salt in a blender and puree until smooth. Pour over the chicken wings and toss to coat. Cover with plastic wrap and refrigerate overnight.

2   The next day, preheat the broiler. Lay the chicken wings on a foil-lined baking sheet. Season with additional salt. Broil until the chicken wings are golden and glistening, 3 to 5 minutes per side. Serve with luscious sliced avocado and more hot sauce.

LEARNING THE ROPES

For a more deluxe dish, substitute your favorite guacamole spiked with hot sauce for the sliced avocado, then dunk the wings in the guacamole before devouring. Holy hell, indeed!

Skewered Chicken

I'm in the Sub-Zero, marinating in soy and sake, when someone calls to me. It's the aloof radish from the crisper that I noticed on my first day.

"Can I help you?" I ask. *What could a radish want from me?*

"No. I just wanted to look at you." Her tone is unnervingly soft. Like me, she's pale, pink, and skinny. But I can see she's wilty and faded now.

"What do you have that I don't?" she asks sadly. And she fades away again into the crowded crisper.

My subconscious rises up before me like a green-eyed ghost. *Fifteen*, she shrieks. *Fifteen previous Ingredients.*

I recall Blades's past. It occurs to me that his other Ingredients have known this marinade, those hands, that burning gaze. I am transfixed by the radish's piercing question: What *do* I have that she hasn't?

glazed chicken skewers with soy sauce and ginger SERVES 2 TO 4

1 pound boneless chicken thigh meat

¾ cup dark soy sauce or tamari

⅓ cup mirin or sweet (cream) sherry

2½ tablespoons sake or dry sherry

1½ tablespoons brown sugar

2 fat garlic cloves, peeled and smashed

¾ teaspoon grated peeled fresh gingerroot

Scallions, white and green parts thinly sliced, for garnish

1 Cut the thighs into 1-inch pieces and place in a shallow dish. Make it beg for the sauce.

2 In a small saucepan, combine the soy sauce, mirin, sake or sherry, sugar, garlic, and ginger. Bring to a simmer and cook for about 7 minutes, until thickened and syrupy. Save ¼ cup of the sauce for dipping and drizzling. When you think they deserve it, pour the remaining sauce over the thighs, cover, and chill for at least 1 hour and up to 4 hours.

3 If using wooden or bamboo skewers, soak them in water for 1 hour. Preheat a grill or broiler. Thread the chicken pieces onto skewers and grill or broil, turning halfway, for about 6 minutes. Serve drizzled with the reserved sauce and showered with scallions.

Jealous Chicken

He has me spread out in parts on a towel while he whips up a marinade. He likes me arranged like this; it means he can spice me up to his kinky tastes. I wonder how his former flames responded to his overbearing ways, and I feel an unwelcome pang.

"What happened with the fifteen past Ingredients?" I ask hesitantly.

He cocks his head to one side and back, surprised. He turns off the blender and gives a resigned shrug.

"Various things. I suppose it boils down to . . ." He pauses, searching for precisely the right word. "Unsuitability."

He helps me into the bowl he's filled with the aromatic green liquid from the blender and massages it into my skin. It makes my flesh come alive, but I can't take my mind off the fifteen. The marinade gives me plenty of time to think.

When he pulls me out I realize I've turned bright green.

"Who was the last one?" I blurt out.

He draws a sharp breath and stills. "Beware, Miss Hen, of jealousy," he intones. "It is the green-eyed monster which doth mock the meat it feeds on."

"Did you quote Shakespeare to her, too?" My voice is shrill.

He runs an anxious hand through his hair.

"No, she was more the earthy type," he sighs. "She did as she was told, and I soon felt we had exhausted the possibilities. Now, are you going to let this go?"

"If you can have nice, pliable Ingredients, why do you need me?"

"I need an Ingredient that forces me to compromise. A cook who isn't compromising is not working hard enough." He grabs the package of foil and tears a sheet off. "You are an exquisitely beautiful bird, Miss Hen. You're smart, savory, and succulent. You've made me change my whole approach to building dishes. Now, do you want to ask more questions, or do you want me to cook you?" His stomach growls, and he smiles that dazzling, predatory smile.

"Cook me, please," I say quietly.

His marinade has worked its magic. By the time he pulls me from the oven I am glowing and mollified, and my green tint has faded—for now—in the golden afterglow of a good, hard cooking.

chicken with horseradish and herbs   SERVES 4

3 garlic cloves, roughly chopped

3 scallions, white and green parts

⅓ bunch of fresh chives

⅓ bunch of fresh flat-leaf parsley

1 lemon, zested and juiced

1½ tablespoons prepared horseradish

1½ teaspoons coarse kosher salt

⅓ cup extra-virgin olive oil, plus more for drizzling

1 (3½- to 4-pound) chicken, cut into 8 pieces, patted dry with paper towels

1   In a food processor or blender, combine the garlic, scallions, chives, parsley, lemon zest and juice, horseradish, and 1 teaspoon salt. Blend for 10 seconds, then add the olive oil and blend until smooth.

2   Nestle the chicken in a bowl and rub gently with the marinade. Cover with plastic wrap and chill overnight.

3   Preheat oven to 425°F. Oil a roasting pan and add the chicken parts. Drizzle with oil, cover the pan with foil, and bake for 20 minutes. Uncover and continue to bake until the chicken is cooked through, about 20 minutes longer. Run the pan under the broiler until the skin crisps, 3 to 5 minutes. That's when to enjoy.

LEARNING THE ROPES

Ever consider a three-way with your ingredients? Serve Jealous Chicken with the Rival Radish Salad (page 156). Or for something less risqué, there's always Taters, Baby (page 156).

Steamy White Meat

S teamy enough?" he asks in a low voice.

I'm unable to answer. Tendrils of vapor rise from my naked, wet breasts. He has cooked me gently but quickly. Kinky as it might be, I find myself wanting more and more from this kitchen Adonis.

He holds a tiny silver spoon above me, letting fall, drop by tantalizing drop, a dark, mysterious dipping sauce. It's the slowest, most sensuous thing imaginable. In her crushed velvet coop my inner goddess fans herself with both wings.

"I'm going to take a very, very long time to season you, baby. I promise you, the sesame sauce is much better this time."

This time? I'm confused. He's never used sesame sauce on me before.

"Better than what?" I manage to say as I catch my breath.

He flushes. "Better than the last time I tested it." It's obvious he's leaving something out. Why would he have tested this sauce without me? Abruptly the specter of the wilty radish fills my mind. I feel the anger rising in my breast. *He made it for her.*

"You've used this same sauce before. With who?" I'm trying not to yell. My inner goddess takes a cold shower and mopes back to her perch to sleep.

"You want an honest answer?"

"Was it her? Was it the radish?"

He inhales sharply, then drops his shoulders with a sigh. "We had experimented with a lot of different permutations. Radish granita, radish tartare, gin radish-tini. Finally, during a radish omakase, I tried her in dipping sauce. I added too much wasabi. It's something I regret very much."

"And you're trying the same thing on me?" I ask coldly.

"No, Chicken. With her it was a yuzu, not rice vinegar, and there was the wasabi. What I've prepared for you is quite different." But he can see he's digging himself deeper. He puts down the tiny spoon.

If I wasn't steamed enough before, I sure as hell am now.

white wine–steamed chicken breasts with sesame oil and scallions   SERVES 4

¼ teaspoon coarse kosher salt

4 boneless, skinless, chicken breasts (about 2½ pounds)

2 cups white wine

1 teaspoon black peppercorns

1-inch-thick coin of peeled gingerroot plus 2 teaspoons grated peeled gingerroot

2 garlic cloves, 1 minced, 1 smashed and peeled

¼ cup soy sauce

2 scallions, white and green parts, thinly sliced, plus more for garnish

1½ teaspoons rice vinegar or white wine vinegar, or to taste

3 tablespoons peanut, safflower, or canola oil

1 teaspoon Asian (toasted) sesame oil

Chile oil or chile sauce (optional)

1 Sprinkle the salt all over the chicken breasts.

2 In a large soup pot set with a steamer basket, bring the wine, peppercorns, gingerroot coin, and smashed and peeled garlic to a simmer. Gently lay the chicken breasts in the steamer basket in one layer, cover the pot tightly, and steam until they are just cooked through, 12 to 20 minutes.

3 Meanwhile, in a small bowl, stir together the grated ginger, minced garlic, soy sauce, scallions, and vinegar, then stir in the peanut oil, sesame oil, and a few drops of chile oil, if using. Slice the breasts thin, then drizzle with sauce and garnish with scallions to serve.

LEARNING THE ROPES

This makes a light and flavorsome meal, but to make it more satisfying, serve the breasts with rice noodles tossed with a little of the sauce and more sliced scallions. Or plain white rice is nice, too.

Bacon-Bound Wings

It's high time I trussed you again, Miss Hen." He flips on the radio and pulls out the outsize spool of twine.

"Maybe I should play hard to get for once," I say coyly.

His eyes widen with surprise and a glint of arousal. He looks me up and down on my cutting board.

"I can't really see how you're going to pull that off."

"It could take more than trussing twine to hold me down tonight."

Katy Perry is belting out "Peacock" from the radio. Not Blades's taste in music at all, which makes it all the sweeter to hear. "Break me off, if you bad, show me who's the boss," Katy chides.

"You are, as ever, challenging, Miss Hen." He gets a foxy look in his eye that sends a thrill of electricity through my insides. "There's more than one way to tie a bird, you know."

"Really, Mr. Blades?" *Holy crap, what have I started?*

From deep in the Sub-Zero he produces a rasher of bacon. He hasn't even touched me, but the sight of the long, pink strips makes my tail tremble.

"Is bacon your answer to everything?" I ask, panting a little.

"It does the trick," he answers, holding a porky lasso a couple of millimeters beyond my reach. He grabs the box of foil and tears off a sheet. I can't stand how arrogant and smug he is right now, but I also can't stand not having that bacon on my skin.

I relent, with a strange, pleasurable sensation suffusing my body.

"Oh, twist my arm," I moan.

maple-glazed wings with bacon SERVES 4 TO 6

¼ cup maple syrup

¼ cup soy sauce

¼ cup chopped scallions, white and green parts

1½ tablespoons rice wine or apple cider vinegar

3 garlic cloves, minced

1 teaspoon freshly ground black pepper

15 chicken wings (about 3 pounds), patted very dry with paper towels

8 strips bacon

1 In a large bowl, combine the maple syrup, soy sauce, scallions, vinegar, garlic, and pepper and mix well. Add the chicken wings and toss them gently so they are bathed in the heady liquid. Cover the bowl with plastic wrap and let the chicken marinate in the refrigerator for at least 2 hours or overnight.

2 Preheat the oven to 450°F. Slice the bacon in half lengthwise to yield long thin ribbons, perfect for restraining your bird.

3 Remove the wings from the marinade and wipe off any clinging garlic or scallion pieces. Tightly tie up each chicken wing in a bacon ribbon and lay the chicken wings, wing tips up and expectant, on a large baking pan. Cover the pan loosely with foil and bake for 30 minutes. Uncover the dish and continue to bake until golden and crisp, another 10 to 15 minutes. Serve hot, using your hands to devour.

Dripping Thighs

The way his apron hangs from his hips already has me all wobbly. But as he coats my thighs with sticky liquid I can hardly contain myself. Is it the wine, or is my aroma starting to drive him crazy, too?

He heats me up fast, and it won't take much to finish me off now. His lips quirk up into a smile. My own juices are mixing with the coating and running all over the place. I get the strangest, sweetest, most hedonistic feeling up and down. It's epicureanism run wild!

He spreads my thighs out on a plate. Sticky hands and at least five wet napkins. What will the housekeeper think? Who cares?

roasted chicken thighs with sweet-and-sour onions SERVES 2 TO 4

1 pound boneless, skinless chicken thighs, patted dry with paper towels

2 garlic cloves, finely chopped

1 teaspoon plus a pinch of coarse kosher salt

½ teaspoon freshly ground black pepper

1 sweet onion, thinly sliced

1 cup white wine

1 bay leaf

1 cinnamon stick

1 tablespoon honey

2 tablespoons unsalted butter

1 Preheat the oven to 450°F. In a large bowl, toss together the chicken, garlic, 1 teaspoon salt, and the pepper.

2 In a small saucepan, simmer together the onion, wine, bay leaf, cinnamon stick, and a pinch of salt until most of the liquid has evaporated, 15 to 20 minutes. Mix in the honey and butter.

3 Spoon the mixture over the chicken and toss well. Spread the thighs, onion mixture, and any juices onto a rimmed baking sheet. Bake until the chicken is no longer pink and the onions are meltingly tender and caramelized, about 25 minutes.

Chicken Strip Tease

I've been prevailed upon in ways I never imagined. I've agreed to everything so far, but now it's my turn. I want more. I want to be dinner, I want to taste like me, I want to be *craved*. He's obsessed with his kinky implements, his techniques, his condiments. I prefer to think this is messed up, but I can see it's the right thing for him. My mind wanders to the fifteen previous Ingredients.

"Your whole control-freak foodie thing, it was because of her, that woman—Mrs. Child." My mood has darkened.

"Julia opened my eyes to many important things," he explains. "In fact, I'd still be eating frozen dinners if it weren't for her."

Frozen dinners? The thought of my poor, fucked-up foodie eating cold Tater Tots as a boy breaks my heart. Not taters, baby, never again!

All right then. I'll bet she never taught you this.

"Strip my breasts, Blades," I command softly. "Now."

His eyes widen. Craving thickens the air around us like a wine reduction. I can tell he's thinking what he might do with my ample white flesh. Well, he's just going to have to think a little longer, because I have to marinate.

So what will it be? Cupped in a warm tortilla? Slicked with vinaigrette? Rubbed up hot with spice?

We won't need a recipe for what we're about to do.

chicken breast strips with balsamic and rosemary SERVES 2 TO 4

1 pound boneless, skinless chicken breasts, patted dry with paper towels

2 garlic cloves, finely chopped

1 tablespoon balsamic vinegar

1 tablespoon chopped fresh rosemary

¾ teaspoon coarse kosher salt

⅛ teaspoon crushed red pepper flakes

3 tablespoons extra-virgin olive oil

1 Cut the chicken into ½-inch-thick strips. In a bowl, whisk together the chicken, garlic, balsamic, rosemary, salt, and red pepper flakes. Lay the chicken into the bowl and turn it gently. Drizzle in 2 tablespoons of oil and turn the mixture again. Wrap the bowl tightly and let the chicken marinate in the fridge for 1 hour or overnight. Pat the chicken dry with paper towels.

2 Place a large skillet over medium-high heat. Add the remaining tablespoon of oil and heat until it is shimmering. Toss in the chicken strips and sear without moving until the undersides are golden brown. Continue to cook, tossing occasionally, until the chicken is just cooked through, about 5 minutes.

LEARNING THE ROPES

Feel free to project your dinner fantasies onto the naked flesh of these well-seasoned breasts. Here are some ideas: wrap in warm tortillas and top with tomatoes, avocado, and grated cheese; toss with salad greens, shaved fennel, and a lemony vinaigrette; cut into smaller strips and fold into an omelet to serve the morning after; shred into chicken soup.

Sticky Fingers

It's just around midnight. He's got me in pieces again, whipping up his latest fancy. Brown sugar and bourbon simmer on the range, smelling juiced up and sloppy. I can't keep up with his shifting moods—sour this morning, sweet tonight. I blame that harpy, Mrs. Child. A cooking show queen, warping boys of just sixteen. Now poor Shifty can't even chew gum without some kind of kinky cookery. Finesse: it's a bitch.

"Is this one of *her* recipes?" I can't hide an edge of bitterness in my voice.

"No, Miss Hen, it's my own preparation. And I wish you'd stop obsessing about Julia. You're flogging a dead horse. She's my past. You are my future."

His future! I let this information soak in. I feel my anger subside slightly and my bones grow warm.

My subconscious is squawking, *You'll get burned again*. I hear her knock on her perch, but I ignore her. She's still got the blues about Mrs. Child and she's got a point, but we've got to move on. How can I resist those deft hands? That godlike mouth and tongue? If the brown sugar doesn't sway me, the bourbon will. Why does it smell so good?

He palms my breast, his fingertips just brushing the sensitive tip. "You fit my hand perfectly, Miss Hen," he murmurs. "Just like a young bird should."

No, I won't let anything come between me and my Shifty Blades. Wild foxes couldn't drag me away.

chicken fingers with brown sugar and bourbon   SERVES 6

1½ pounds boneless, skinless chicken breasts, patted dry with paper towels

1 teaspoon pure chile powder

1 teaspoon ground cumin

1 teaspoon coarse kosher salt

½ teaspoon freshly ground black pepper

2 tablespoons brown sugar

2 tablespoons honey

1 tablespoon bourbon

Extra-virgin olive oil, for drizzling

Freshly squeezed lemon juice, for drizzling

1 Using a sharp knife, trim the breasts lengthwise into 1-inch-wide fingers.

2 In a medium bowl, combine the chile powder, cumin, salt, and pepper. Add the chicken fingers and mix well until thoroughly coated. Cover the bowl with plastic wrap and let marinate in the fridge for at least 1 hour, or longer if you want to make the chicken wait for it.

3 Preheat the broiler. Oil a large baking pan or a broiler pan. In a small saucepan, bring the brown sugar, honey, and bourbon to a boil, stirring. Pour half the mixture over the waiting chicken, tossing it gently. Drizzle with oil.

4 Lay the fingers out on the pan without crowding, and broil, turning once, until the chicken is sticky all over and browned around the edges, 5 to 7 minutes.

5 Brush the chicken with more of the sticky glaze for serving, then drizzle with lemon juice.

Thighs Spread Wide

I must have you right now," he says breathlessly, throwing me down and opening my thighs on the first surface he can find.

"On this?" I ask. "Isn't this a baking sheet?"

"It'll have to do." He practically roasts me with his burning gaze as a low growl issues from his gut.

He looks down at me and slips his fingers between my thighs, spreading them wide. He begins a slow and sensual assault with his hands, scattering capers and lemon everywhere. Because I can't close my legs, it's intense, really intense. *Oh fucking my . . .*

roasted chicken thighs with mushrooms

SERVES 4 TO 6

1½ pounds boneless, skin-less chicken thighs, patted dry with paper towels

1 teaspoon coarse kosher salt

¼ cup chopped fresh oregano

2 tablespoons freshly squeezed lemon juice

2 garlic cloves, minced

½ teaspoon freshly ground black pepper

8 ounces cremini mushrooms, trimmed and quartered

⅓ cup extra-virgin olive oil

2 to 3 teaspoons capers

2 tablespoons white wine, chicken broth, or water

Chopped fresh flat-leaf parsley, for garnish

Lemon wedges, for serving

1 Season the chicken with the salt. In a large bowl, combine the oregano, lemon juice, garlic, and pepper. Add the chicken and mushrooms to the bowl and toss to coat. Drizzle in the oil and stir well. If you can bear waiting, let marinate for up to 4 hours in the fridge, or for 15 minutes at room temperature while the oven preheats.

2 Preheat the oven to 500°F.

3 Spread the chicken thighs open in the bottom of a 9 x 13-inch baking pan. Scatter the mushrooms and capers around and over the chicken. Add the wine, broth, or water to the pan and roast until the chicken is golden around the edges, glistening with juices, and just cooked through, about 25 minutes.

4 Sprinkle with parsley and serve with lemon wedges, for squeezing.

Chicken Thighs, Stirred Up and Fried Hard

I lie exhausted on a bed of rice. He leans over me, tasting me and savoring the juices that are still dripping from me. Cab Calloway is shimmying away on the stereo. Blades runs a hand through his hair and flashes a grin at me.

"Satisfied, Miss Hen?"

I mumble my assent. Holy cow, where does he get his energy? This is the third time we've cooked today. Doesn't he have some kind of job?

"Is stir-fry like this for everyone? I'm surprised anyone ever goes back." I smile, remembering.

"I can't speak for everyone, but it's damn good with you." He sucks on another piece of my warm flesh.

But I can tell he's already thinking of how to top this. He's layering flavors in his head, mixing textures. He can't just stop and enjoy, he's got to find a way to move it to the next level. He's already made a delicious dish, can't he be happy with that?

From the stereo, Cab is crooning, "Chicken ain't nothing but a bird." Right now I'm hardly even that. Blades can finesse all he likes, I think as I drowse. I need my beauty sleep.

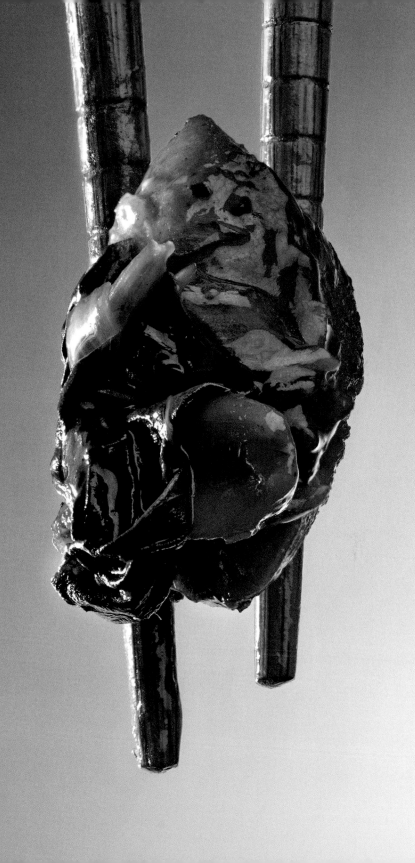

stir-fried chicken with spinach and peanuts
SERVES 4

1 pound boneless, skinless chicken thighs, patted dry with paper towels

½ teaspoon coarse kosher salt

½ teaspoon freshly ground black pepper

⅓ cup low-sodium chicken broth

1½ tablespoons soy sauce

1½ teaspoons cornstarch

1 teaspoon honey

1½ tablespoons peanut oil

1½ teaspoons Asian (toasted) sesame oil

1 bunch scallions, chopped, white and green parts separated

2 garlic cloves, finely chopped

1 tablespoon grated peeled fresh gingerroot

⅛ teaspoon crushed red pepper flakes

4 cups baby spinach

½ cup unsalted roasted peanuts

Cooked rice, for serving

1 Cut the chicken thighs into easy-to-nibble-size pieces; season with the salt and pepper. In a small bowl, whisk together the broth, soy sauce, cornstarch, and honey.

2 Heat a large skillet over medium-high heat. Add the peanut and sesame oils and let heat for 30 seconds. Stir-fry the chicken hard, fast, and furiously until it's golden and nearly done, 5 to 7 minutes. Scoop the chicken onto a plate and make it beg you to finish it off.

3 Add the scallion whites, garlic, ginger, and red pepper flakes to the pan. Cook until fragrant, about 30 seconds. Add the spinach and stir-fry for 1 minute longer.

4 Stir the broth mixture into the skillet and gently heat to a raucous simmer. Scrape up the browned bits from the bottom of the pan and let the sauce bubble until it is thick and velvety, 1 to 2 minutes. Stir in the peanuts, the waiting chicken, and the scallion greens. Toss until the sauce reaches its desired thickness and the chicken is quite done, 1 to 2 minutes more. Enjoy over rice.

Hashing It Out
the Morning After

I begin to wonder whether I'm up to the standard of his singular tastes. Lately, finesse seems to require mayonnaise, fish sauce . . . and this morning there's a bottle of ketchup waiting next to the Wolf. I know it will displease him, but I have to ask. *Here goes nothing.*

"Do we always have to use a condiment?"

He runs his hand through his hair, which still has that amazing just-cooked look from last night. He cocks his head from side to side and frowns.

"Condiments are for your own protection. Some of the other ingredients can be rather strong, and we need to balance the flavors. And it lubricates you."

"Don't you ever want to just taste me *au naturel*?"

He closes his eyes as if searching for strength.

"Your savor is always present, Chicken. I choose flavors to enhance your taste, not cover it."

"Couldn't you leave me undressed, just once?" I feel myself gaining the upper hand for once.

"All right, Miss Hen," he sighs with resignation. "This morning the condiment is optional. You don't need it anyway." He adds, "Even if the other Ingredient could use it."

Other Ingredient? What's he up to now?

"You're pairing me?" I ask suspiciously.

"Yeah, baby." He quirks his lips into a crooked smile. "Taters."

chicken hash with sweet potatoes   SERVES 4

1¼ pounds sweet
potatoes, peeled and
diced into ½-inch cubes

4 tablespoons unsalted
butter

1 teaspoon coarse kosher
salt

¼ teaspoon freshly ground
black pepper

1 small onion, chopped

1 small green bell pepper,
seeded and diced

2 garlic cloves, minced

2 cups cooked, diced
chicken meat

Pinch of crushed red
pepper flakes

2 scallions, white and
green parts sliced, for
garnish (optional)

Fried eggs, for serving
(optional)

Ketchup, for serving
(optional)

1 Bring a large pot of water to a boil and add the
sweet potatoes. Par-cook until halfway done, about
5 minutes. Drain, then spread out on a clean dish towel
to dry.

2 Melt half the butter in a large skillet and add the sweet
potatoes and half the salt and pepper. Let cook without
stirring, until the potatoes brown on one side, then turn
and brown well on the other side, about 10 minutes.
Transfer to a plate.

3 Add the remaining butter to the skillet and sauté the
onion, bell pepper, and garlic until tender and golden
around the edges, about 7 minutes. Add the chicken
and crushed red pepper flakes and sauté until the
chicken starts to brown. Return the potatoes to the pan
and sauté until everything is well mixed and golden,
taking care not to crush the potatoes too much.

4 Serve the hash topped with scallions and a fried egg
and ketchup on the side, if you like.

Go Get the Butter Breasts

What is this?" I ask, horrified. The machine is sleek and silver and rather beautiful. It has a big gift bow on it. I stare at it blankly. *How can this possibly be for me?*

He smiles proudly. "This, Miss Hen, is your new in-chamber vacuum sealer."

Sealer? "I like the packaging I came in," I say weakly.

"That plastic sack," he says with distaste, "is an amoeba playground. It's not safe. I've disposed of it. This machine has an anaerobic gas flush that will protect you and keep you from spoiling."

"I'm perfectly fresh as I am." I had enough trouble with the fancy spices, and now this? Why is he such a control freak?

"You are quite fresh. But you've been looking thin, Miss Hen. You look like you've lost five ounces, possibly more, in the last two days. I told you, I need you juicy, and to be juicy you must preserve your water and fat content."

He thinks I'm scrawny. And maybe even spoiled. My inner goddess flips him the bird. Let him watch his own damn fat content. I know there will be hell to pay, but I cluck audibly.

"No, I can't accept this," I cluck.

His eyes darken. He looks at me with that intense gaze that makes me feel agonizingly self-conscious. *Am I too lean?*

"Very well," he says quietly.

"Don't be angry with me."

His expression is hooded, halfway between fury and something else. I long for him to put his hands on me, and I can see him staring hungrily at my breast. My vitals ooze with raw desire.

"You are a most disobedient Ingredient, Miss Hen." He quirks his mouth into a crooked smile.

He grabs a sheet of foil. *Oh yes.* I know he won't let me win that easily, and that what's coming next will be rough and hot. Longing lubricates my nether parts.

I'm too lean for you? *Nothing a stick of butter won't cure.*

sautéed chicken breasts with aromatic brown butter and hazelnuts   SERVES 2 TO 4

1 teaspoon coriander
  seeds

2 boneless, skinless
  chicken breasts (about
  8 ounces each), patted
  dry with paper towels

1 teaspoon coarse kosher
  salt

¾ teaspoon finely grated
  orange zest (from
  1 small orange)

¼ teaspoon freshly ground
  black pepper

¼ teaspoon freshly grated
  nutmeg

2 tablespoons unsalted
  butter

2 tablespoons chopped,
  toasted hazelnuts or
  almonds

1 Using a mortar and pestle, or the flat side of a knife, crush the coriander seeds and put them into a bowl.

2 Using the side of a rolling pin, gently pound the breasts until they submit, flattening them ¼ inch thick. Put the chicken into the bowl with the coriander and add the salt, orange zest, pepper, and nutmeg and toss to coat. Let marinate in the fridge for at least an hour, or better, up to 6 hours.

3 Melt 1½ tablespoons of the butter in a very large skillet over medium-high heat and let it simmer until it turns golden brown and starts to smell nutty. Add the chicken in batches and cook until golden on both sides, about 3 minutes per side. Transfer the chicken to a platter and tent with foil to keep warm.

4 Melt the remaining ½ tablespoon butter in the pan and add the nuts. Let them heat up and crisp until very fragrant, 1 to 2 minutes. Serve on top of the breasts.

Red Cheeks

He pulls two small red orbs from his jacket pocket.

Holy shit! What are those for?

"Apples," he says. "I thought we might play with these tonight."

"While you cook me?" I'm shocked. They're awfully big.

My inner goddess looks up from her yoga magazine, google-eyed, and starts kegeling madly.

He nods slowly, his eyes darkening. I've learned to be apprehensive when he brings me fruit.

"Will you season me after?"

"No."

For a second, I register a tiny stab of disappointment. He chuckles.

"You want me to?"

I hesitate. I just don't know. What used to feel wrong now feels so right.

"Well, tonight you might just have to beg me."

Oh my.

"Do you want to play this game?" he continues, holding up the apples. "You can always take them out if it's too much."

I consider my position. He looks so roguishly tempting—unkempt hair from recent cooking, dark eyes dancing with gastronomic thoughts, his lips raised in an amused smile.

My inner goddess is already on her knees in supplication, still kegeling and ready to beg for forbidden fruit.

"Yes."

It's a relief, actually. Finally a pair of red cheeks that aren't mine.

roasted chicken thighs with apples and cinnamon   SERVES 4

2 small red apples, cored
  and cut into 1-inch
  cubes
1 pound boneless, skinless
  chicken thighs, cut into
  2-inch-wide pieces
2 tablespoons vermouth
2 tablespoons cold butter,
  cut into cubes
2 garlic cloves, minced
½ teaspoon ground
  cinnamon
½ teaspoon coarse kosher
  salt
½ teaspoon freshly
  ground black pepper

Crusty bread, for serving

1 Preheat the oven to 425°F. Core the apples and cut into 1-inch cubes.

2 On a large, rimmed baking sheet, toss together all the ingredients except the bread. Roast until the chicken is cooked through and the apples are softened, 20 to 25 minutes. Serve with the copious pan juices, with the crusty bread for dunking.

Pound Me Tender

It's Mrs. Child, isn't it?" I ask, horrified. On the cover of the cookbook is a woman of a certain age, wielding a huge mallet, gleefully about to bring it down on what appears to be a half-eaten chicken. *Why can't that crazy woman leave well enough alone?*

He closes his eyes for a moment.

"It's her," he says as he opens them again. He's glowering at me now. *Uh-oh.* I can't stop now.

"That culinary cougar warped your palate at such a tender age." It's because of her that I feel so imperfect, so dull. She set his standards too high for a mundane fowl. How can I ever measure up?

"You don't understand. She was an early inspiration, but that was long ago. I create my own preparations now."

Then why am I staring at her cookbook right now? I keep quiet, nearly shaking with despair. But I have so many questions waiting to burst out.

"Fine, Miss Hen. Let's cook without a recipe, shall we?" He shoves the cookbook to the side and lays me out on the butcher block. As always his fingertips find my softest, most delicate parts.

"How do you want to be cooked? Well? You tell me!" His tone is simultaneously challenging and vulnerable.

I take up his challenge.

"Show me how you'd use that," I say. His eyes widen at my audacious choice. Slowly he picks up the rolling pin at the tip of my outstretched wing.

He drives the heavy pillar into my most sensitive flesh, gently but insistently. The effect is shattering. Jeez, he really is in great shape. My flesh lights up with the pain and secret exhilaration.

My subconscious gives up. She needs a drink.

With the last blow I can contain myself no longer. A plume of raw chicken juice escapes me, hitting the cookbook and spattering Julia in the face. *Oops!*

My subconscious smirks and smugly dips her beak into her dirty martini.

crispy chicken tenders with cashews and coconut curry   SERVES 4 TO 6

1¼ pounds chicken tenders, patted dry with paper towels

½ teaspoon coarse kosher salt

¼ teaspoon freshly ground black pepper

½ cup coconut milk

1 tablespoon red curry paste

½ teaspoon Asian fish sauce or soy sauce

¾ cup roasted, salted cashews

¾ cup unsweetened coconut flakes

¾ cup cornflakes

Lime wedges, for serving

Cilantro sprigs, for serving

1 Preheat the oven to 450° F. Lightly grease a large baking sheet.

2 Using the side of a rolling pin, gently pound the chicken tenders into submission; they should be ¼ inch thick. Season with the salt and pepper.

3 In a wide, shallow bowl, whisk together the coconut milk, curry paste, and fish or soy sauce.

4 In a food processor, pulse together the cashews and coconut flakes until finely chopped. Add the cornflakes and pulse until just blended. Transfer to another wide, shallow bowl.

5 Dip a chicken tender in the coconut mixture, letting the excess drip back into the bowl. Then dip the chicken in the cashew mixture, turning to coat evenly. Transfer the chicken to the prepared baking sheet. Repeat with the remaining chicken.

6 Transfer the chicken to the oven and bake, turning once halfway through, until golden all over, about 10 minutes total. Serve with lime wedges and cilantro.

LEARNING THE ROPES

Tenders are indeed the most tender part of the bird, but you can use boneless skinless breasts cut into ½-inch-wide strips. The pounding is optional, depending upon how much your chicken wants it.

Inner Green Goddess Chicken Salad

I marvel at how much I have I've endured—and yes, relished—at those god-like hands. The obscure spices, the laborious preparations, the oohing and aahing over flavors built and textures manipulated, even the recipes with their fussy food-porn photos. It's all so twisted, but it's so him. Now it feels so me, too.

My inner goddess dresses herself in a rich, verdant velvet, and spreads herself languorously on a California King–size bed of arugula.

And yet, he's so fucked up. He claims to respect me, says I'm the most beautiful Ingredient he's ever known, but he acts as if the beauty of the food were not enough. Why does he always have to take it to some other level? Where will it end?

My subconscious clucks at me, arms crossed over her breast. *Why are you grilling yourself like this? You've made your bed.* I pull a face at her. Yes, I have, willingly. I want him to lay me down on that leafy bed every night of every week.

That's the bottom line. I want to belong to his appetite, to answer his cravings. My inner goddess sighs with relief. It occurs to me that she has a rather small brain, but thinks instead with the moister parts of her anatomy.

"He's my happy ending," I whisper. I will be his.

My inner goddess, lounging deliciously on her arugula bed, smiles placidly and returns to her romance novel.

chicken salad with green goddess dressing

SERVES 4

½ cup sour cream

¼ cup tightly packed watercress leaves

3 tablespoons mayonnaise

2 garlic cloves, roughly chopped

1 anchovy fillet (optional)

1 tablespoon chopped fresh chives

1 tablespoon chopped fresh flat-leaf parsley

1 tablespoon chopped fresh basil

1½ teaspoons freshly squeezed lemon juice

½ teaspoon coarse kosher salt

¼ teaspoon freshly ground black pepper

3 cups shredded, cooked chicken meat

Greens or bread, for serving

Toasted sliced almonds, for serving

1 In a blender, combine the sour cream, watercress, mayonnaise, garlic, anchovy if using, chives, parsley, basil, lemon juice, salt, and pepper. Blend until smooth and green.

2 Combine the chicken with enough of the dressing to richly coat it and toss well. Serve the chicken salad over greens that are drizzled with the remaining dressing and sprinkled with almonds, or make it into sandwiches with your favorite bread.

LEARNING THE ROPES

This inner green goddess dressing is also lovely as a dip. Serve it in a bowl surrounded by chips, cut-up veggies, and, if you like, cold slices of cooked chicken.

Whipped Livers

The door of the Sub-Zero opens, revealing a kitchen filled with people nibbling on canapés and sipping wine. *Ooh, a party.* I'm relieved for once not to be the main course.

Blades appears distracted, chatting with his guests as he reaches for more canapés. Odd, there aren't any canapés in here. Before I know what's happening, he reaches discreetly inside me and pulls out my giblets. *Now?*

He deftly slides my liver out of its paper envelope, while appearing to focus on his conversation with a talkative fellow holding a napkin.

"Blades, what are you doing?" I whisper urgently.

He doesn't answer, but looks around the room smiling benignly. He continues to fondle my liver with his fingertips until I can't stand it.

He gently places my quivering offal into a skillet where some softened onions are waiting for me. *Holy fucking shit . . .* we're cooking in the middle of a party? Everyone's mingling and chatting, but I am not paying attention. He stirs my insides with a deft wooden spoon, around and around. . . .

I squirm and gasp as I feel a hardening in my heated organ.

"Always so ready, Miss Hen," he whispers. I make a low hiss of longing. How can he do this with all these people here?

He nonchalantly carries my blushing liver to the food processor. *Oh . . . how long will he keep escalating this?* It makes me feel so—dirty.

He pulses the machine a few times, whipping me into a soft frenzy. My insides dissolve in ecstasy, my mind a spiral of pure sensation. I can't hold it together any longer.

B'gawk, I groan as his long finger continues to hit the pulse button. I'm thankful that the room full of people seems completely oblivious.

He appears to be perfectly composed. This isn't fair. He calmly spoons me onto toast and takes a long, slow bite, from which it takes me several minutes to recover.

"I can't believe you just did that," I giggle.

"You'd be surprised what I can do, Miss Hen."

No, nothing about Shifty Blades surprises me anymore.

chicken liver crostini SERVES 6

¼ cup extra-virgin olive oil

1 small yellow onion, peeled, halved, and thinly sliced

1 pound chicken livers, patted dry with paper towels and cut in half crosswise

½ teaspoon coarse kosher salt

¼ teaspoon freshly ground black pepper

2 tablespoons cream sherry or port wine

½ tablespoon chopped fresh rosemary leaves

6 slices country bread, toasted

Sea salt, for garnish

1 Heat the oil in a large skillet over high heat, then add the onions and let them get brown and oh so tender, about 12 minutes.

2 Add the chicken livers and salt and pepper and reduce the heat to medium; cook until the quivering insides of the livers have lightened from crimson to rosy, about 5 minutes. Using a slotted spoon, transfer the livers to a food processor.

3 Turn the heat to high and add the sherry to the skillet with the juices. Cook, scraping up the browned bits, until the juices have thickened, 1 to 2 minutes. Stir in the rosemary.

4 Scrape the mixture into the food processor. Pulse to whip the livers until they are just broken up, but still chunky and wanting more. Spoon the liver mixture over the toast. Sprinkle with sea salt, and consume.

Blushing Parts

He gives me a conflicted look. My poor Shifty Blades—a domineering home cook who at heart is still a teenager struggling to make a decent bowl of Froot Loops, who feels unworthy of the gastronomy he sees in books and on TV . . . my lost foodie. . . it's heartbreaking.

"Sorry about Julia," he murmurs.

"I know you feel like you need her and all her recipes and advice. But I don't think you do. I think you can make your own decisions without her."

"You're right," he says quietly.

Whoa! Breakthrough.

"Really? No Mrs. Child?"

"No more."

He lays me down in parts on a soft layer of berries. I try to collect myself and let this information infuse. The memory of the time he first cooked me on a bed of cherries fills my mind. That was an eternity ago.

"You are the most beautiful, toothsome, versatile, and cookable food I've ever had the good fortune to create with. You've never failed me, Chicken. I can't imagine a meal without you."

What? What is he saying? My skin flushes bright red.

"I want to taste you every day of every week. I want you to be more than my Ingredient. I want you to be the center of everything I do from now on. I crave you, Miss Hen."

"Are you asking me what I think you are?"

"Chicken, will you be my Specialty?"

cranberry baked chicken with apple cider

SERVES 4

---

1 cup apple cider

½ cup dried cranberries

2 tablespoons apple cider vinegar or white wine vinegar

1 cinnamon stick

1-inch slice peeled fresh gingerroot, smashed with the flat side of a knife

½ teaspoon freshly ground black pepper

3 pounds bone-in, skin-on chicken parts, patted dry with paper towels

1½ teaspoons coarse kosher salt

2 tablespoons cold butter, cut into pieces

Cooked wild rice, quinoa, or couscous, for serving

1 Preheat the oven to 450°F. Combine the cider, cranberries, vinegar, cinnamon stick, and ginger in a saucepan over medium-high heat, and season with the pepper. Bring the liquid to a boil. Lower the heat and simmer until the cranberries are very soft and the liquid is reduced by two-thirds and has a syrupy consistency, about 20 minutes. Discard the cinnamon stick and ginger.

2 Season the chicken with the salt. Lay the parts in a roasting pan, skin side up. Spoon the cranberry mixture over the parts, then dot with the butter. Roast until the chicken parts are browned around the edges and cooked through, about 40 minutes. Serve up with rice, quinoa, or couscous, and enjoy.

LEARNING THE ROPES

You can make this with all white meat (choose bone-in breasts) or all dark meat (choose thighs and/or drumsticks). Or use a mix of parts and satisfy chicken lovers of all inclinations.

three

Birds Gone Wild

Advanced Techniques

He's holding a long, detailed contract. *Holy shit.*

"The publisher sent the paperwork this morning. My recipes won them over immediately."

I think I'm in shock. I try to imagine how readers would react to . . . what Blades does. To me. Surely the general public would find it too strange, too dark, too twisted.

He smiles his sly smile. "They want my cookbook badly. And they're going to give me a lot of money for it. Especially since I turned them down the first time."

Turned them down?

"What changed your mind?"

"You did, Chicken. They wanted me to cover all kinds of dishes and Ingredients. But it's not about Ingredients for me anymore—it's about my Specialty. This book isn't just my cookbook. It's yours, too. It's our baby."

Our baby. Our Little Booklet!

He shows me the email:

Chef,

Your chicken recipes are most singular. We have a deal.
We believe your cookbook could be huge.
Let's discuss the details in person. I'd like to observe you at work if I may.
Congratulations!

Best,
W

C. Wiley
Editor, Swann Publishing

Observe Shifty at work? Oh boy.

"And just how do you intend to put your kinky cookery into words? Isn't it a little advanced for general consumption?"

"Miss Hen, we've only scratched the surface. We haven't yet started on the advanced techniques." His eyes blaze with that secret fire.

My tail twitches and desire blossoms in my body.

"Is tying me up an advanced technique?" I ask hopefully. My inner goddess kisses her wing tips for luck.

"Maybe one part," he says, "But your role as my Specialty will require more elaborate preparation. We'll be layering entirely new flavor profiles. There will be special equipment. It's time I show you the toy drawer."

"You're going to play with your food?" I cluck sweetly.

"No, Miss Hen," he says, giving me a menacing look.

He reaches under the counter to pull open a deep drawer containing what looks like a voodoo doctor's kit. In meticulously ordered slots are assorted mallets and shears, some soft brushy things, a bunch of colored loops that look like rubber bands, a giant spool of twine, a baster with a needle at the end, and an iron bowl from the center of which extends a shockingly long, black prong.

I stare dumbly at its impressive length, hypnotized.

Come Hither Chicken

Oh, baby, I don't need this," I say.

My limbs are bound tight to my body, the trussing twine just tight enough to dig into my flesh without breaking the skin. Just how I've come to like it. What's bothering me is the butter.

It glistens in the bowl he's holding out to me, wafting the narcotic, deliciously indecent aroma of truffles. My pulse starts racing. *Shit* . . . How can he do this with just a smell?

"*I* need this," he says with conviction.

Why? Why does he need these extravagant things? Does he feel inadequate? Am I inadequate? Why spend so much?

"No, Shifty," I say, "you don't. I'm your Specialty now, you've made me yours. You don't have to keep proving yourself. I'm the luckiest Ingredient in the world."

"No, Chicken, I'm a lucky cook. You've changed the way I do absolutely everything. But now that you're my Specialty, you'll just have to get used to some minor luxuries like this. Besides," he continues, "it counts as an advanced technique."

As he talks I continue to fall under the exotic spell of the truffles. His heated gaze makes my juices start to run clear. At this point I can think of nothing but my need to be slathered in that butter.

Oh, well then, as long as it's an advanced technique . . .

roasted chicken with truffle butter SERVES 4

1 (3- to 3½-pound) chicken, patted dry with paper towels

1½ teaspoons coarse kosher salt

¼ teaspoon freshly ground black pepper

1 tablespoon safflower or canola oil

2 tablespoons white or black truffle butter

Chopped fresh chives, for serving

Mashed potatoes, for serving (optional)

1 Preheat the oven to 375°F. Massage the chicken all over with salt and pepper, remembering to pay special attention to her cavity. Using butchers' twine, truss her up nice and tight, following the directions on page 34. The tighter, the better.

2 Heat an ovenproof skillet over medium heat, then add the oil and let heat for 20 seconds. Lay the chicken in the pan on her side and let brown for 5 minutes, adjusting the heat as necessary so she doesn't burn. Flip and repeat on the other side.

3 Lay the chicken on her back, transfer to the oven, and roast her for 20 minutes. Add the truffle butter to the pan and continue to roast, basting with the fragrant butter, until her thigh juices run clear and she is enticingly golden all over, about 25 to 35 minutes longer. The more you baste, the more succulent she will be. Serve with the pan juices and the chives, over mashed potatoes if you like.

LEARNING THE ROPES

If you can't find truffle butter with which to lavish your bird, use regular butter. After cooking, if you like, slowly drizzle her with truffle oil. Or leave her as she is, juicy and golden.

Spatchcocked Chicken

Holy shit, he's wearing that apron, and he's reaching into the back of the toy drawer.

I want it, oh yes. And he wants me. I get it now. The hungry look on his face, the growling of his stomach like I was the last *amuse bouche* on earth. But *this*—I don't know if I can do what the recipe demands. Yet, this is what he does—he hurts food to make it taste good. This is what I signed on for. If I want my Shifty Blades, I have to be ready for anything.

"I want it," I say. *I belong to you.*

He turns me over so I can't see what he's doing.

"I'm going to spread you out. I'm going to open you up. I'm going to take you places you never knew existed." I can feel his manic anticipation.

His skilled hands have me completely at his mercy. As he opens me up a shock ripples through me, and it's a sweet, strange, voluptuous feeling. He lays me breast-up on the pan, flatter than poultry should be. This is unnatural, it can't possibly be as pleasurable as it is. But the warmth of the pan penetrates me so evenly. I feel melty, juicy, exquisitely yummy.

Now I know why they call it spatchcocking.

butterflied roasted chicken with herb and almond pesto SERVES 2 TO 4

1 (3½- to 4-pound) chicken, patted dry

1½ teaspoons coarse kosher salt, plus a large, firm pinch

4 scallions, white and green parts roughly chopped

1 cup roughly chopped tender fresh herbs, such as a combination of dill, basil, flat-leaf parsley, and cilantro

½ cup sliced almonds

¼ cup extra-virgin olive oil, plus more for the roasting pan

2 tablespoons freshly squeezed lemon juice

1 garlic clove, chopped

½ teaspoon freshly ground black pepper

Lemon halves, for serving (optional)

1 Using large, strong kitchen shears and a confident hand, forcefully cut the backbone out of the chicken; first cut along one side of the backbone, then cut along the other side until it releases, then pull it out. Gently spread the bird open, pressing down on the breast to flatten it (see Learning the Ropes). Massage the flesh with 1½ teaspoons of salt.

2 Whirl the scallions, herbs, almonds, oil, lemon juice, garlic, and pepper together in the blender until quite smooth and luscious. Taste and season with a large pinch of salt. Smear the pesto all over the bird. Cover and refrigerate for at least 4 hours and preferably overnight.

3 Preheat the oven to 450°F. Spread the bird flat, breasts up, in an oiled roasting pan. Roast until golden and succulent, 40 to 50 minutes. Let rest for 10 minutes, then have your way with her, squeezing on lemon juice if she needs a tang.

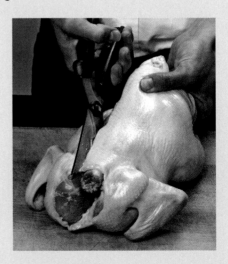

LEARNING THE ROPES

If you're dealing with a novice bird, have your butcher butterfly your chicken for you. He or she will be happy to oblige.

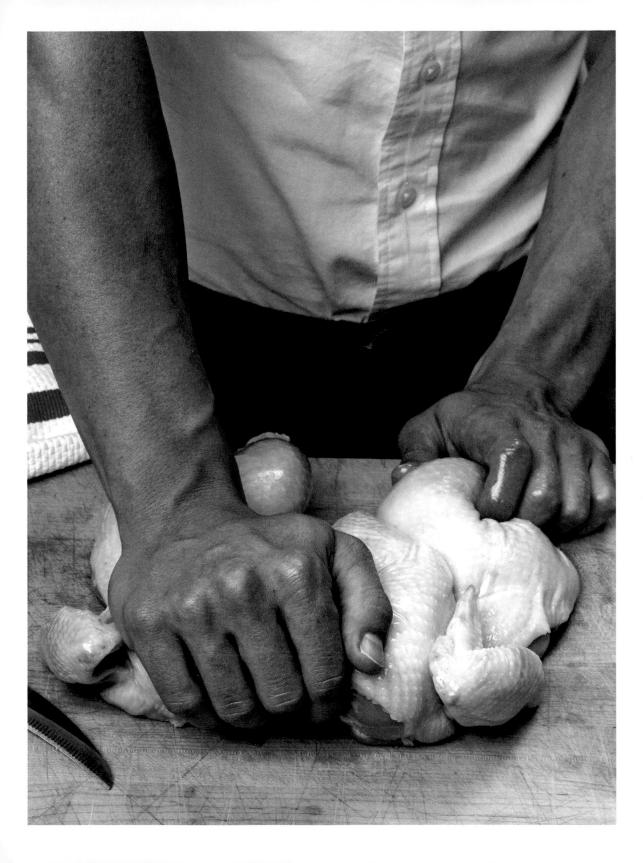

Erect Chicken

I'm eyeing the black bowl, with its startling black prong. My inner goddess's eyes are bugging out of her head. Even she's unsure. *Jeez, I could never . . .*

"How does that work?" I ask, fascinated.

"The vertical roaster? It holds you up while I cook you. Do you want me to show you?"

"Yes. I'd like a home demonstration."

"Very well, Miss Hen. You are, as ever, highly unpredictable."

He starts with an unhurried massage across my breast and legs, his hands traveling my body until they reach the apex between my thighs.

"You are a daring and beautiful bird," he continues. "I'm going to put this inside you now. Are you ready?"

"Yes," I whisper.

He hoists me up over the bowl and lowers me slowly onto the upright prong. I gasp as its majestic length fills me, holding me tightly in position. The sensation is excruciating and exquisite. Am I really ready for this?

"This will be intense, because you'll be unable to shift as I cook you." He reaches down to bind my feet with a length of twine. I am utterly immobilized. Just before he delivers me to the tender mercies of the oven, I feel him scatter some objects at my feet. Stuck as I am, I can't tell what they are.

"Taters, baby," he says, with his uncanny way of reading my mind.

I hardly hear him as the oven heat takes possession of my flesh. I stiffen a little and my legs pull almost painfully against the twine, but I hardly notice. This is the most agonizing, exquisite feeling. My juices surge as flavor detonates up and down my body.

He pulls me off of the device, frees my ankles, and lays me gently on the bed of potatoes. My legs unbend a little and my juices flow over my golden, glowing skin.

That was, without a doubt, the most intensely juicy finish we've ever achieved together. Hmm, the upright roaster . . .

Note to self: explore the toy drawer more often.

vertical roasted chicken with spicy tomato potatoes   SERVES 4

1 (3½- to 4-pound) chicken,
   patted dry with paper
   towels
2¼ teaspoons coarse
   kosher salt
¼ teaspoon freshly ground
   black pepper
3 tablespoons extra-virgin
   olive oil
1½ pounds Yukon Gold or
   russet potatoes, cut into
   1-inch dice
2 tablespoons tomato paste
1 teaspoon ground cumin
½ teaspoon hot chili
   powder
¼ teaspoon freshly grated
   nutmeg

LEARNING THE ROPES

Cooking bands, which
look like colorful rubber
bands, are reusable and
can withstand the heat
of your oven. Use them
in place of twine to tie
up your chicken's legs if
she's in the mood to flash
a little color or if you
don't want to use twine.

1   Preheat the oven to 425°F. Massage the chicken all
    over, including the cavity, with 1½ teaspoons of the salt
    and the pepper. Rub a tablespoon of the oil all over the
    chicken's skin.

2   Position the chicken's nether parts over the vertical
    roaster's erect member and thrust the bird down. Tuck
    her wing tips up behind her wings, behind her body.
    Tie her legs together with a piece of butcher's twine or
    cooking bands (see Learning the Ropes). If the vertical
    roaster is too small to hold all the potatoes in the
    bottom, place the roaster and potatoes in a 9 x 13-inch
    baking pan.

3   In a bowl, toss together the potatoes, tomato paste,
    cumin, chili powder, nutmeg, the remaining 2 table-
    spoons oil, and the remaining ¾ teaspoon salt. Scatter
    the potatoes on the bottom of the pan around the
    chicken.

4   Roast for 30 minutes, then stir and baste the potatoes
    with some of the rendered chicken fat at the bottom of
    the pan. Continue to roast until the skin is golden and
    the thigh juices run clear when pricked with a knife, 10
    to 20 minutes longer. The potatoes should be soft. Let
    the chicken rest for 10 minutes before serving.

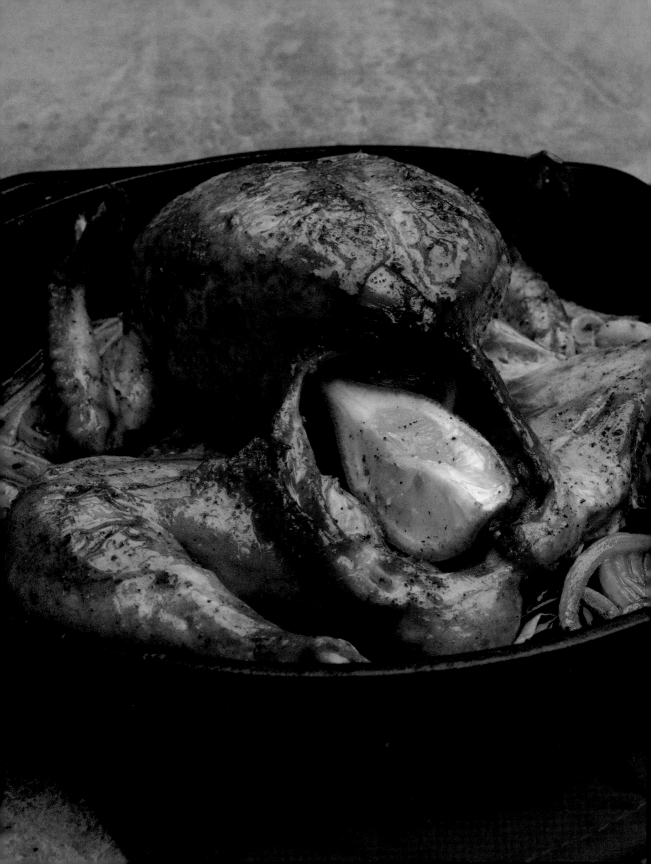

Spread-Eagle Chicken

You seem a little on edge." he says.

On edge? Me? I can't help but squirm after the stretching he gave me last night with the upright roaster. My inner goddess is stuck in pigeon pose as she attempts a yoga routine.

"Let me relax you," he continues in a low voice. "Take a deep breath, Chicken. Think of a waterfall." He positions me on my back on a cutting mat, in a neutral position. He grasps one of his many blades and traces a gentle line, drawing the tip toward the apex of my thighs, down *there*. I feel vulnerable and eager as my legs loosen. His expert hands do the rest, coaxing my legs wider, wider, until they slacken and drop to the mat. I am indecently splayed, yet so blissed out I scarcely register his fingers sliding into me, until I feel a deep clenching where he's inserted half a lemon. *Oooooh*.

"You look beautiful like this, Chicken. I must take a moment to enjoy the view." The hunger in his voice makes my body hum with endorphins and a dark feeling I'm afraid to name. In my fading consciousness I see my inner goddess arching into something like a slutty upward-facing bow. Inner peace is clearly not what's on her mind.

"Now—" he says quietly, "let's kick it up a notch." He fiddles with the stereo remote and abruptly cranks up some throbbing hip-hop, jolting me awake. With an oven mitt he pulls a hot, heavy skillet from the Wolf. Wow, I can feel its torridness as he brings it closer—it's not just hot, it's solar. "Drop It Like It's Hot" thumps out of the kitchen speakers like a tendering mallet. But I'm still too limp to do anything but moan softly.

"Oh, Chicken, you're so ready," he yells over the noise.

He slips me into the oven and cooks me ardently and fast. Somehow, despite the conflagration around me, a tiny, unnoticed drop of calm expands inside me, filling me as relentlessly as the citrus did before. As the heat and thudding bass line crisp every inch of my outside, a juicy serenity swells within. *Holy shit . . . it's intense . . . and deep . . . the music . . . my juices are building so quickly . . .* It's as if all the toys and techniques we've ever used were only leading me step-by-step to this poultry nirvana. The crispiness and juiciness come together at exactly the same time, and every part of my body finishes in unison. *Ahhhhh*.

My inner goddess, languid and wet in corpse pose, wears a beatific smile. *Om shanti shanti shanti.*

skillet-roasted chicken with golden onions and lemon SERVES 4

1 (4- to 4½-pound) whole chicken, patted dry with paper towels

2 teaspoons coarse kosher salt

½ teaspoon freshly ground black pepper

1 lemon, quartered

1 tablespoon extra-virgin olive oil

1 onion, thinly sliced

1   Firmly rub the chicken inside and out with salt and pepper, paying special attention to the cavity. Let it rest uncovered at room temperature while the oven preheats.

2   Place a large cast-iron or other heavy ovenproof skillet in the oven and let it preheat at 450°F for 45 minutes.

3   Transfer the chicken to a cutting board. Using a sharp knife, cut the skin connecting her legs to the rest of the body. Use your hands to spread open the thighs until you feel the joint pop. Place 2 of the lemon wedges inside the chicken.

4   Carefully transfer the chicken, breast side up, to the hot skillet. (Use oven mitts whenever handling the pan.) Press down on the legs so they rest flat on the bottom of the pan. Drizzle the bird with the oil. Roast for 25 minutes. Toss the onion slices into the bottom of the skillet. Stir to coat with the pan juices. Roast for 10 more minutes; stir again. Continue cooking until the onions are tender and the chicken's thigh juices run clear, 5 to 15 minutes more (for a total cooking time of 40 minutes to 1 hour).

5   Serve the chicken with the pan juices and onions, seasoning everything with juice from the remaining lemon wedges, if desired.

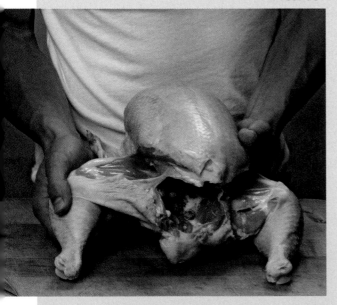

Safeword Fowl

What I'm about to do to you will be very intense. I'm counting on you to guide me. What are the safewords, Chicken?"

"Golden," I mumble, "if I'm approaching doneness."

"And?" he prods, making his eyes hard.

"Black, if I'm in danger of drying out."

"Good." He flips on the Wolf and starts to rub my breast with salt and pepper. My skin comes alive as his hand travels down my sternum, down there. He slips two deft fingers inside me, tracing circles with tantalizing slowness. I flinch as he pushes something smooth and bulbous into me. *Oh my.*

"Garlic cloves," he breathes. "And herbs. They'll make your finish more powerful."

He lays me forward on a roasting rack, leaving my most vulnerable part exposed and throbbing, then thrusts me into the wild heat of the Wolf. The heat works me fast and hard, bringing me to the edge. My insides pulse and tense, but just as my juices start to flow freely, he lowers the heat. *Holy shit, he's teasing me.*

He pulls me out and I can hear the rip of the foil. He flips me roughly onto my back, jarring and thrilling every part of me. Then he covers me in a sheet of foil and turns his back. *How long is he going to make me wait?*

Finally he comes back, a little smile quirked up on his lips, his breathing ragged.

"Do you have any idea how delicious you are?" he pants.

"Finish me," I manage to gasp out in a low, heated voice.

He pushes me onto the rack and throws me back into the oven's high heat. Deep inside me the cloves pulse and I clench around them involuntarily. My skin crisps as hot juices pound through my body. *Gah!*

"Golden!" I scream, "Golden! Golden!"

roasted chicken with tomatoes, garlic, and tarragon SERVES 4

1 (3½- to 4-pound) chicken, patted dry with paper towels

1½ teaspoons coarse kosher salt, plus more to taste

¼ teaspoon freshly ground black pepper, plus more to taste

1 bunch of fresh tarragon, leaves chopped, stems reserved

5 smashed and peeled garlic cloves

2 tablespoons unsalted butter, softened, plus 2½ tablespoons cubed

1 large cut ripe tomato, diced into 1-inch cubes

½ cup low-sodium chicken broth or water

¼ cup dry white wine

2 tablespoons tarragon or white wine vinegar

1 Preheat the oven to 500°F. Massage the bird all over with salt and pepper, including inside the cavity. Stuff the chicken with the tarragon stems and garlic. Rub the chicken with 2 tablespoons of softened butter, sprinkle with 2 teaspoons of chopped tarragon, and season generously with more salt and pepper.

2 Lay the chicken breast side down on a rack in a flame-proof roasting pan, and roast for 20 minutes. Reduce the temperature to 325°F. Thrust a wooden spoon into the cavity of the bird and flip it over so it's breast side up. Continue to cook for another 25 minutes. Transfer the chicken to a plate, cover loosely with foil, and set aside. Turn the oven back up to 500°F.

3 Take the roasting rack out of the pan and set it aside. Place the roasting pan on top of the stove over medium-high heat. Add the tomatoes, chicken broth or water, wine, tarragon vinegar, and 2 tablespoons of the chopped tarragon; bring to a boil. Use a wooden spoon to scrape the bottom and sides of the pan, loosening the caramelized juices. Let boil until the mixture is thickened and saucy, 5 to 8 minutes.

4 Whisk the remaining 2½ tablespoons of butter into the sauce. Place the roasting rack back in the pan and put the chicken back on the rack, breast side up. Pour any juices that have collected on the plate into the pan. Return the pan to the oven for 10 to 15 minutes, basting every 5 minutes, until the thigh juices run clear. Serve the chicken blanketed with the sauce and garnished with more of the tarragon.

Hog-Tied and Porked Chicken

I'm sitting with the formerly enormous ham next to the Wolf. She takes in the stainless surfaces and the thick hobs.

"And to think he can work this thing."

"Mm-hmm."

"That's kinda hot."

"Yeah, I think so."

We laugh giddily together.

It's so long since we really had a chance to catch up. I'd forgotten how much I love to hang out with her. Shifty's brother has had a slimming effect on her figure, with his constant appetite. But before I can chide her about the profusion of nibble marks on her backside, she zeroes in on my ankles.

They have deep, brown marks left by the trussing twine, where Blades forgot to cover them. I can't believe he's left these marks on me. The ham grows suspicious.

"What happened to you? What the hell is that deviant doing to you?"

Man, if she only knew. *Oh, he just porked me with a Spanish sausage, bound me up with twine, and roasted me silly. And that's not to mention the black iron prong he put up my orifice.* I could feed her some cock-and-bull story about food handling and safety precautions. But I can't possibly tell her about the chorizo—she'd freak.

Instead I try the patented Shifty distraction trick.

"I have news. We're coming out with a cookbook."

"What?" She's blown away. "When does it come out? That's fantastic!"

Whew, it worked.

"Thanksgiving!" My voice wobbles with excitement.

"Oh, Chicken, I couldn't be happier for you. But seriously, you'd better get rid of those marks before you pose for the pictures."

Pictures? Holy crap.

trussed roasted chicken with
chorizo stuffing   SERVES 4

2 tablespoons extra-virgin
   olive oil
½ pound fresh chorizo
   sausage
½ cup finely chopped
   onion
1 cup day-old bread, torn
   into pieces
1 (3½- to 4-pound)
   chicken, patted dry with
   paper towels
1½ teaspoons coarse
   kosher salt
1½ teaspoons freshly
   ground black pepper

1 Warm 1 tablespoon of the oil in a large skillet until
   shimmering. Using your hands, firmly squeeze the
   casing of the sausage, letting the fresh meat spill into
   the pan (discard casing). Add the chopped onion.
   Cook, breaking up the meat with a fork, until it is golden
   brown and the onions are tender, about 7 minutes. Toss
   in the torn bread pieces, making sure they are evenly
   coated with the spicy juiciness.

2 Preheat the oven to 400° F. Pat the chicken very dry,
   including the cavity. Rub the skin with the remaining
   1 tablespoon oil. Season the chicken inside and out
   with the salt and pepper. Take a generous handful of
   the chorizo mixture and plunge it deep into the cavity.
   Pack the cavity loosely; you want it to feel full but not
   overwhelmed. Reserve any remaining stuffing to bake
   alongside in a ramekin.

3 Cut two generous lengths of kitchen twine. With the
   first, lash together the legs at the ankles, crossing the
   twine several times before securing with a double knot.
   Secure the second around the length of the chicken's
   body, pinning its wings closely to its sides. You don't
   want it to move at all or leak any stuffing.

4 Place the chicken on its back on a rack set over a
   rimmed baking sheet. Roast until the thigh juices run
   clear and the skin is crisp and golden, about 45 minutes
   to 1 hour. Cover with foil and let rest for 15 minutes
   before carving.

LEARNING THE ROPES

If you can't find chorizo,
a fresh, spicy uncured
sausage, a hot Italian
sausage will do the job
just as well. The hotter,
the better.

Coquettish Croquettes

Blades comes into the kitchen with a guy in a pale brown shirt, stone chinos, and small hoops in each of his large ears. He's long and slim, with cavernous dark eyes. His hair is scruffy and looks oddly unkempt, and he has a desperate, hungry look.

It's our editor, Wiley.

"So this is the bird?" His eyes seem to bulge from their sockets.

Blades tenses. "Yes, this is my chicken." His voice makes it clear who rules this roost.

Wiley cocks his head to either side in a disturbingly familiar way. "I'd like to take a few photos while I'm here. Purely for reference, of course."

Blades's expression darkens momentarily.

"Photos," he mumbles. "Well, we'll have to see about that."

The idea of being photographed makes me incredibly nervous. Illustrations maybe. I had imagined diagrams. But photos? Jeez, I hope this recipe doesn't make my butt look big.

Blades ushers Wiley out and returns with a sigh of relief.

"Well, Mr. Blades, are we alone?" I coo.

"I believe you are entirely defenseless, Miss Hen."

I find myself once again stretched out on the cool granite of his sleek countertop.

I've never seen anyone move a knife so fast and sure. He passes it so smoothly into me, I hardly know it's happened until I fall apart in a crisp heap. I groan, reveling in the sensation as he corrals me with a deft nudge of the tip of his knife. He's earning his nickname tonight.

crunchy chicken parmesan croquettes

MAKES ABOUT 1½ DOZEN CROQUETTES

2½ cups shredded cooked chicken

¼ cup extra-virgin olive oil

1 small onion, finely chopped

2 garlic cloves, finely chopped

¼ teaspoon freshly grated nutmeg

Pinch of cayenne pepper

¼ cup all-purpose flour

1 cup whole milk

¼ teaspoon coarse kosher salt, plus more as needed

¼ teaspoon freshly ground black pepper

2 large eggs

¾ cup plain bread crumbs

⅓ cup grated Parmesan cheese, plus more for serving

¼ cup finely chopped fresh flat-leaf parsley

Safflower or canola oil, for frying

Lemon wedges, for serving

1 Using a steady knife and a disciplined hand, finely chop the chicken meat (you can also pulse it in the food processor until minced).

2 Heat the oil in a large skillet over medium heat. Add the onion and cook until softened, about 5 minutes. Stir in the garlic, nutmeg, and cayenne. Cook for 1 minute. Stir in the flour, then gradually whisk in the milk; season it with salt and pepper. Simmer for 3 minutes, stirring occasionally, or until the mixture is thick and bubbly. Scrape the mixture into a bowl and fold in the chicken; let cool. Taste and add more salt if needed. Cover and refrigerate until chilled, at least 1 hour.

3 Using moist hands, form the mixture into 18 equal-sized egg-shaped croquettes (each about 2½ inches across).

4 In a wide, shallow bowl, beat the eggs with 3 table-spoons water. In a separate dish, combine the bread crumbs, cheese, and parsley. Dip each croquette in the egg mixture, then coat with bread crumbs and transfer to a platter.

5 Fill a small pot halfway with oil and heat to 365°F. Fry the croquettes in batches, turning twice, until golden brown, about 3 minutes. Transfer to a paper towel–lined plate to drain. Serve immediately, with lemon wedges and more grated cheese on top.

Chicken Under the Covers

Wiley is staring hungrily at my legs. He reaches out a tentative hand. Blades sets his mouth in a hard line. "Wiley . . ." he says menacingly.

Wiley backs off in dismay. "Excuse me. I didn't mean . . ."

Blades carries me over to the other counter.

"I don't like you exposing so much flesh on camera," he hisses under his breath to me. "That's a hard limit for me."

Clearly he hasn't grasped the whole idea of food photography.

"How do you expect to get pictures for our cookbook?" I ask. "I'll have to show myself. Legs. Breast. The whole enchilada."

"Perhaps, Miss Hen," he says dryly. He turns around and stalks off to the pantry. *That's it?* My Shifty doesn't usually give up so easily. Wiley waits quietly.

A few minutes later Blades comes back carrying a ball of dough—and a rolling pin. *Oh my, what's he going to do with that?*

He uses it to roll out the dough. *Oh.* I'm a little disappointed.

He places me in a deep, round baking dish. So far so good. He takes strips of dough and lays one gently across me. Then another, and another.

Holy fuck. He's hooding me with crust. I see him smirk just before he covers me over completely. The bastard.

"Now you may shoot the bird," he says. I hear Wiley start to click away.

Inside the solid crust I'm steaming up.

LEARNING THE ROPES

If you aren't comfortable with crust bondage, skip it; instead, arrange the crust on top of the pie. Tuck the edges into the side of the pan and slash the center to allow steam to escape. Novices can purchase a prepared pie crust instead of making their own.

creamy chicken pot pie SERVES 6 TO 8

FOR THE CRUST

10 tablespoons unsalted
  butter, ice cold

1⅓ cups all-purpose flour

¼ teaspoon fine sea salt

1 to 3 tablespoons ice-cold
  water, as needed

FOR THE FILLING

4 tablespoons unsalted
  butter

2 medium leeks, rinsed and
  thinly sliced

2 medium potatoes, peeled
  and diced

1 small turnip, peeled and
  diced

1 carrot, peeled and diced

1 celery stalk, peeled and
  diced small

1 garlic clove, chopped

½ teaspoon dried thyme

¼ cup all-purpose flour

2 cups unsalted chicken
  broth

½ cup heavy cream, plus
  more as needed

¾ teaspoon coarse kosher
  salt

½ teaspoon freshly ground
  black pepper

2 cups shredded cooked
  chicken

½ cup fresh or frozen peas

1 To make the crust, slice the butter into cold cubes. Toss together the flour and the salt in a large bowl. Work the butter into the flour until the mixture forms pea-size crumbs. Slowly dribble in the water until the dough just combines together. Wrap tightly in plastic wrap and refrigerate for at least 1 hour.

2 To make the filling: Melt the butter in a large skillet over medium heat until it is sizzling. Add the leeks, potatoes, turnip, carrot, and celery. Cook, stirring often, until the vegetables are slightly caramelized, 7 to 10 minutes. Stir in the garlic and thyme; cook for 1 minute. Toss in the flour and stir vigorously to coat the mixture with the flour; let it cook for 1 minute. Stirring constantly, pour in the broth in a slow, steady stream, then do the same with the cream. The sauce should come together smoothly. Season it with salt and pepper. After the mixture has bubbled and thickened for a few minutes, stir in the chicken and peas. Remove the pan from the heat and let it cool completely.

3 Preheat the oven to 375°F. Spoon the filling into a 9-inch deep-dish pie plate or a 2-quart soufflé dish.

4 To prepare for pie bondage, lightly dust a large work surface with flour. Roll the crust out to a 10-inch circle. Using a sharp knife or pastry wheel, slice the crust into ½-inch strips. Arrange the strips over the chicken in a tight, restraining, crisscross pattern, covering up all the chicken underneath. Brush the top lightly with cream. Bake until the crust is golden and the filling is hot and bubbly, about 45 minutes. Let cool slightly before serving.

Roast Me All Night Long Chicken

Black, Black!" I whimper. "Please."

The door of the Wolf flies open and he pulls me out, the roasting pan cradled in his oven mitts.

"No," he gasps. "You can't be overcooked. What have I done?" He scrambles for a meat thermometer.

I begin to sob uncontrollably. No, I'm not overdone, but I was beginning to fall apart. I had to use the safeword.

It started in the usual way, with me facedown on a rack. He slipped a lemon inside of me, and another, then some garlic and herbs, filling me over and over. Then he cooked me, low and slow. At first it was sweet and warm and I built slowly. My flesh softened and practically separated from my bones. But he wouldn't bring me to doneness. Hour after hour, for how long? How many hours would he keep this up? Was he angry because of the photos? This wasn't cooking, it was revenge. Finally I broke.

"Why are you taking so long?" I ask plaintively.

"Chicken, slow roasting is a standard technique in . . . I just had to . . ." He stills and hangs his head. "I'm sorry," he whispers.

I begin to recover myself. In fact I'm still quite tender and moist.

"You just had to what?" I ask.

"I just had to cool you down for another round," he says finally. He quirks his lips into a foxy smile. *Hell's bells.*

"You've already made a meal of me. Have you come back for more?" I ask, quickening.

He drizzles me with oil and then cranks up the heat. I feel my legs start shaking. The stove is quaking. My heart is aching.

Oh, Blades, roast me all night long.

slow-roasted chicken   SERVES 4

1 (3½- to 4- pound)
  chicken, rinsed well and
  patted dry with paper
  towels
1½ teaspoons coarse
  kosher salt
½ teaspoon freshly
  ground black pepper
1 lemon, halved
2 sprigs of fresh rosemary
2 bay leaves
6 garlic cloves, smashed
  and peeled
1 tablespoon extra-virgin
  olive oil

1 Rub the chicken all over with the salt and pepper,
especially inside the cavity. If you want to draw this
out even more, let the bird marinate in the fridge,
uncovered, all day long (4 to 8 hours).

2 Preheat the oven to 200°F. In a baking dish, gently lay
the chicken down on her breasts. Squeeze the lemon
juice all over her and then thrust the squeezed-out
lemon halves into her cavity along with the rosemary,
bay leaves, and 2 of the garlic cloves. Scatter the
remaining garlic in the bottom of the pan. Cover tightly
with foil and roast her long and slow, all night long, for
8 hours. (Or start your bird in the morning and serve
for dinner.)

3 Take the chicken out of the oven and turn on the broiler.
Unwrap the bird and use two spatulas to move her to
a waiting platter. Take care; after her night, she might
just well fall apart (then you know you did a good job).
Drain off any liquid that accumulated in the bottom of
the pan (save this stock for another use). Discard the
bay leaves. Move the chicken back to the pan, breast
side up. Drizzle with the oil and broil until the breast is
golden brown and the chicken can't take it anymore,
2 to 4 minutes longer. Let the chicken rest for at least
5 minutes, then devour. You won't need a knife; the
meat will fall off the bones at your very touch.

Backdoor Beer-Can Chicken

I might have been killed," Blades says darkly.

Oh no no no. Not my Shifty. Control-freak foodie obsessive, master of the kitchen, my boy with his toys. I can't imagine a world without him.

"The igniter on the oven misfired. I was preheating it, but it never lit. The gas knob jammed. Fortunately I always keep a toolbox in the kitchen. It was sheer luck I wasn't suffocated or blown up."

Wiley looks sidelong at Blades.

"Hmm, yes. Very fortunate." He fidgets anxiously.

"All right, disaster was averted. We'll grill outside. Wiley, if you'll excuse me, I'll get things prepped."

He carries me out to the grill, where I finally break down.

"Oh, Shifty," I sob.

"Hush," he says. He smiles and holds up a beer can.

"Yes, baby, have a drink. I'm sure you need it."

"Oh, no, this is not for me, Chicken." He quirks his mouth into a wicked smile.

Holy fuck . . . Will it? How?

I gasp as he fills me with its astonishing girth. The feeling of fullness is overpowering.

He rests me on the grill and I can feel the entire world start to engorge. Desire explodes in my cavity like a hand grenade.

I perceive Wiley hanging back, seemingly texting, his hungry eyes fixed on me in this compromising position. I can just make out the title of the book sticking out of his jacket pocket—*How to Cook a Wolf.* Hmm.

Just before awareness evaporates, I recall my mom's warning—never hire a coyote to guard the henhouse.

grilled beer-can chicken with cajun mayonnaise   SERVES 4

1 (3½- to 4-pound) chicken, patted dry with paper towels

1½ teaspoons coarse kosher salt

½ teaspoon freshly ground black pepper

1 cup mayonnaise

1½ tablespoons Cajun spice mix or hot chile powder

Hot sauce, to taste

1 can beer

Lime wedges, for serving

1 Prepare the grill for indirect heat: if using gas, turn on half the grill to medium high, leaving the other side off, and let preheat for 10 minutes. If using charcoal, mound and light the coals under one side of the grill only. Place an empty disposable foil baking pan on the empty side of the grill to catch drips. (You can also line the empty side of the grill with foil; do so before you heat the grill or use mitts.)

2 Rub the chicken all over, inside and out, with the salt and pepper. Mix the mayonnaise with the spices and hot sauce. Massage all but 2 tablespoons of the mayonnaise mixture all over the chicken, including the cavity.

3 Open the beer and drink (or pour out) half of it. Lower the chicken over the beer can so it penetrates the chicken cavity. The chicken should be straddling the can, balancing it. Place the chicken on the unlit side of the grill and cover the grill. Let the chicken cook for 60 minutes.

4 Check the chicken; if the skin isn't brown enough, move the chicken to the other (lit) side of the grill or just turn the gas on under the chicken. Cover the grill and let cook until the chicken is cooked through (the thigh juices will run clear and the skin will be golden). The whole thing should take about 1¼ hours but it could vary depending on your grill. If the coals start to burn down, replenish them as needed.

5 When the chicken is done, carefully remove the beer can (hold the chicken with tongs and use an oven mitt to pull out the can). Let the chicken rest for 5 minutes before carving. Serve with lime wedges.

Flame-Licked Chick

I'm marinating deeply. Turmeric, garam masala, and ginger penetrate into my dreams. I'm not even sure I'm awake when the door of the Sub-Zero opens on to a dark kitchen. Awareness floats just out of reach like a dancing firefly.

I seem to see predatory eyes glowing dimly in the darkness, staring at my yogurt-smeared flesh. Recognition creeps up my spine. *Wiley?*

He gets out a camera and starts snapping pictures of me in my marinade.

"That perverted prep-cook hasn't outfoxed me," he grumbles to himself. "He thinks this is all about him and his little recipes. But I think big. Fast food is where the big bucks are. The foodie's ideas just need to be scaled up. Tray of sticky fingers, bucket o' dripping thighs. And I'm just the guy to do it. I'm going to make that bird mine. And if he tries to pick a bone with me about that, I've got these compromising pictures!

"Not bad for a kid from the hardscrabble highways of Monument Valley," he continues. "It's been the same all my life. People constantly underestimating me. Just a guy who reads books. Hah! A guy who reads books, who happens to be an inventor and a *super-genius*. I was out there chasing birds before that kid could even make ramen. Sure I never got one, but I never give up. They always laughed at me. But now this little cook-tease is my ticket to Fat City.

"That maniac and his bird will both get what's coming to them. And I'll get what's mine."

He finishes shooting and places me back in the fridge.

The marinade-induced delirium fades. It was just so vivid. What if it wasn't a dream? *Our Little Booklet!* I feel a tingling of danger. But the powerful Indian spices are stronger than danger, and they penetrate deeper than panic.

grilled chicken with tandoori spices

SERVES 4 TO 6

1 (3½- to 4-pound)
chicken, cut into
8 pieces and patted dry
with paper towels

1½ teaspoons coarse
kosher salt

Juice from 1 lime, plus
wedges for garnish

1 cup whole-milk yogurt

1 small red onion, peeled
and coarsely chopped

1 large jalapeño or small
serrano pepper, seeded
if desired, sliced

2 garlic cloves, peeled and
smashed

1-inch-thick slice of peeled
fresh gingerroot,
coarsely chopped

1 tablespoon ground
garam masala

½ teaspoon ground
turmeric

1 tablespoon safflower or
canola oil

Cilantro leaves, for
garnish

1   Using a small, sharp knife, slash each chicken piece
through the flesh until you reach the bone. One slash
is plenty for the smaller pieces; slash the larger pieces
twice. This allows the marinade to penetrate fully and
deeply so the chicken can take it all in.

2   Rub the chicken pieces all over with the salt and lime
juice. Refrigerate for 20 minutes so the chicken can
recover.

3   Meanwhile, add the yogurt, onion, jalapeño, garlic,
ginger, garam masala, and turmeric to a blender
and puree until very, very smooth. Pour the yogurt
mixture over the chicken pieces, tossing to coat them
thoroughly, and refrigerate for at least 8 hours and up
to 24 hours.

4   Preheat the grill or broiler. Wipe the marinade off the
chicken with paper towels and then lightly brush the oil
all over the flesh. Grill or broil, turning once, until the
pieces are charred at the edges and the thigh juices run
clear, 25 to 35 minutes (the breasts will be done before
the legs and wings). Devour with cilantro and lime
wedges for garnish.

LEARNING THE ROPES

**Broiling these succulent pieces is a
messy affair. Either use a broiler pan
or line a rimmed baking sheet with
oiled foil to keep the juices at bay.**

Chicken Sub

I stare blankly at the laptop screen, stunned. It's filled with the image of my breast, half-covered in melted mozzarella, up close and in living color.

Holy shit! Was the dream real? I suspected Wiley was sneaking photos but I thought they were cookbook photos. Not this shocking, lurid food porn.

"Um, I seem to be on Google," I manage to croak. Blades is slicing a tomato on the counter behind me.

"Everyone's on Google, babe," he says, distracted. "That's the point of Google."

"But . . . in a fast-food ad?"

He whips around to the laptop and stares, transfixed by the images of my white meat laid out on a bun and spattered with cheese. I recall Wiley's hungry eyes and his last words—*I'll get what's mine.*

"Seems someone else wants to specialize in chicken," he mutters as he rushes to the phone. Oh boy, is he angry.

He barks terse instructions into the phone. "I want his ass fired . . . Blackmail? Yes, he stole the recipes, my recipes . . . I want the photos removed too. Inform the fast-food chain I took the precaution of secretly copyrighting everything. They'll grasp the situation at once." He looks up at me and I see his face change from agitation to something else—a look of carnal craving.

"Keep me posted," he snaps and puts away the phone, still staring at me. I sit frozen on the platter as he shrugs on his apron, ties it around his hips in that way, and struts over to me.

His eyes are scorching as he unsheathes a considerable length of baguette. *Oh my.*

"Those photos were obscene," he breathes. "But on the other hand . . ."

I melt with a mixture of relief to have escaped the clutches of that blackmailing coyote and anticipation of that long baguette. Maybe food porn isn't such a bad thing after all.

Beep beep! My inner goddess zooms down an endless highway into the sunset, ecstatic and alive.

chicken submarine sandwich
with mozzarella   MAKES 6 SERVINGS

---

6 tablespoons extra-virgin
olive oil

1½ tablespoons freshly
squeezed lemon juice

1 tablespoon chopped
fresh tarragon or thyme
leaves

2 garlic cloves, minced

1 teaspoon grated lemon
zest

Coarse kosher salt and
freshly ground black
pepper

12 chicken cutlets (about
2½ pounds)

2 medium-size ripe
tomatoes, thinly sliced

¾ pound fresh mozzarella,
thinly sliced

6 submarine rolls (or
8-inch lengths of
baguette or Italian
bread), split and toasted

Butter, as needed (the
more the better)

½ cup chopped fresh basil
(optional)

1 In a large bowl, whisk together 3 tablespoons of the
oil, the lemon juice, tarragon, garlic, lemon zest, and a
large pinch of salt and pepper. Transfer 1½ tablespoons
of the dressing to a small bowl and set aside. Add the
chicken to the remaining dressing in the large bowl
and let marinate at room temperature for 30 minutes,
or cover and refrigerate for 4 hours or, even better,
overnight until it begs for you.

2 In a medium bowl, toss the tomato slices with the
reserved lemon-herb dressing and let sit while you
cook the chicken.

3 When the chicken can no longer stand the anticipation,
heat the remaining 3 tablespoons oil in a large skillet
over medium-high heat. Gently wipe away any clinging
bits of garlic from the bird's soft flesh, and season the
cutlets with salt and pepper.

4 Working in batches, sear the chicken, without turning,
until golden on one side, 2 to 3 minutes. Top each cutlet
with some of the cheese. Cover the pan and cook until
the cheese has melted and oozed all over the cutlets
and the chicken is quite done, 1 to 2 minutes more.

5 Grease up the toasted rolls liberally with the butter. To
assemble the sandwiches, place 1 cutlet on the bottom
half of each roll. Top with some of the tomato, then
a sprinkling of basil, if using. Repeat the layering of
chicken, tomato, and basil; cover each sandwich with
the top half of the roll.

Sexy Sliders

lap! Smack! Whack!

He has me in his twitchy palms, kneading me vigorously and slap-ping me into patties. Each smack of his hand pushes me closer to the edge of my limits.

"Ow!"

"Stamina, Chicken," he says in a low voice.

It's not the whacking. I've come to crave the safe, warm feeling I get after a good licking. It's the aromatics that are heating me up.

After all we've been through, after all the hot and saucy things he's done to me, at heart I still long to look like myself, to feel like myself, taste like myself. Despite his talk of ingredient expression, he still seems to be hung up on expressing spices through me.

"Ow! We need to talk."

He stills his hands, and his expression clouds. I'm no longer afraid of Shifty's moods, but it still makes me pause.

"I can't take this, night after night," I explain. "These strong flavors are wearing me out."

His face looks pained. "You're leaving me?"

He still doesn't get it? I feel exasperation welling. "No, you big paranoid fussbudget. I want the chance to express myself. I want the freedom to be *me*." I wonder how he feels about losing the cookbook deal. *Oh, Little Booklet.*

"These flavors are part of what makes us work so well." He says this with conviction, but his eyes look vulnerable and slightly scared. Is he really afraid I won't stick around? Poor, messed-up foodie. *No, stand your ground, Chicken.*

"I want more. I want you to want me for my tasty dark meat and succulent white meat. I want you to crisp my skin."

"I know, hearts and flowers, a big china platter and a carving knife. And then what? Taters, baby?"

I give up. "Stop kidding around and cook me already."

"Chicken, do you know you're delicious when you're angry?"

chicken sliders with thai flavors and sriracha mayonnaise   SERVES 2

1 pound ground chicken, preferably a mix of light and dark meat

1 tablespoon chopped fresh Thai or regular basil

1 tablespoon Asian fish sauce

1 tablespoon finely grated peeled fresh gingerroot

1½ teaspoons light brown sugar

1 lime, zested and juiced

2 scallions, white and green parts, chopped

2 garlic cloves, finely chopped

1 serrano pepper, seeded and finely chopped

½ cup mayonnaise

2 teaspoons Sriracha or other hot sauce, or to taste

2 tablespoons peanut, safflower, or canola oil

6 slider buns

Sliced tomato, for garnish

Sliced avocado, for garnish

Thinly sliced red onion, for garnish

Kosher salt, to taste

1   In a large bowl, massage the chicken with the basil, fish sauce, ginger, brown sugar, lime zest, scallions, garlic, and serrano pepper until she's thoroughly inundated with them. In a separate bowl, whisk together the mayonnaise, lime juice, and Sriracha.

2   Form the chicken into 6 equal-size patties (each about ¾ inch thick). Heat a large skillet over medium-high heat. Add the oil. Cook the patties until the meat is just cooked through, 3 to 4 minutes per side.

3   Spread some of the mayo mixture on the inside of each slider bun and top with burgers. Garnish with tomato, avocado, and red onion. Sprinkle with salt. Enjoy with plenty of napkins.

Chicken with Hearts and Flowers

I'm at rest under a big sheet of foil. My legs and breast are warm and relaxed. My skin is perfectly crisped, my insides are still tingling where his fingers seasoned me. Jeez, does he know how to roast a girl.

I'm slightly suspicious, though. He hasn't spiced or flavored me, just a quick bath in citrus. This isn't the Shifty Blades I've come to expect.

"Ready?" he asks. There's something different in his voice.

He whisks the sheet off me with a flourish, and I'm struck completely speechless.

There, in front of me, awaits a china platter garlanded with the most beautiful flowers I've ever seen. The table is set with exquisite china and silver flatware. Sweet music is playing on the stereo, the Dixie Chicks, I think. A flute of Cristal glistens in the candlelight. On another plate is a heap of garnishes topped with hearts of palm.

"You wanted hearts and flowers," he says shyly.

I can't believe he's done this.

"Here are the hearts . . . " He pulls over the plate of hearts of palm.

"And these are the flowers," I whisper, finishing his sentence. "Oh, Blades, it looks delicious."

"I think it will be wonderful in our cookbook," he murmurs. There are tears in his eyes.

Little Booklet? "I thought the contract was canceled after your editor stole your recipes, blackmailed you, and tried to blow you up."

"I had another publisher up my sleeve. You don't think I'd put all my eggs in one basket, do you?"

My Shifty, my Chef. I know deep down I will always be his and he will always be mine.

roasted chicken with hearts of palm, avocado, and orange salsa SERVES 4

Zest of ½ orange

2 tablespoons freshly squeezed orange juice

Zest of 1 lime

2 teaspoons freshly squeezed lime juice

2 garlic cloves, minced

1 teaspoon dried oregano

1¾ teaspoons coarse kosher salt

1 teaspoon freshly ground black pepper

2 tablespoons extra-virgin olive oil

1 (3½- to 4-pound) whole chicken, patted dry with paper towels

HEARTS AND FLOWERS SALSA

4 oranges, peeled and diced

2 avocados, peeled, pitted, and diced

1 (7.8-ounce) can hearts of palm, drained and chopped

¼ cup chopped red onion

2 jalapeño peppers, seeded and finely chopped

2 teaspoons freshly squeezed lime juice

Coarse kosher salt

Edible flowers, for garnish

1 In a bowl, whisk together the orange and lime zests and juices, garlic, oregano, ¾ teaspoon salt, and ½ teaspoon pepper. Whisk in the oil.

2 Season the cavity of the chicken with the remaining 1 teaspoon salt and ½ teaspoon pepper. Place the chicken in a large bowl. Pour the marinade over the chicken and turn it slowly, until it is completely bathed in marinade. Chill it, covered, for 1 hour.

3 Preheat the oven to 400°F. Place the chicken, breast side up, in a large roasting pan. Roast until the juices run clear when a sharp knife is thrust into the deepest part of the thigh, about 1 hour to 1 hour and 15 minutes. Let the chicken rest for 10 minutes.

4 While the chicken rests, prepare the salsa. In a bowl, fold together the oranges, avocados, hearts of palm, onion, jalapeños, lime juice, and a large pinch of salt.

5 Carve the chicken into pieces and arrange on a large platter. Spoon the salsa over the chicken and strew the flower blossoms over the plate.

Happy Ending Chicken

I could get used to this china platter. And Shifty seems to enjoy the Cristal. We can afford it now that our cookbook is out. It's become bigger than we ever dreamed, and ebook sales are skyrocketing. We still visit the toy drawer, but Blades has found ways to satisfy himself without it.

Tonight it's a little French number. He massages butter under my skin, mixed with herbs that smell of the South of France. Then he ties me up and roasts me gently and completely. The butter is so silky and wet. It brings out the essential me, without the fancy dressings and luxurious sauces.

He sighs. "I just love chicken."

"I love you too, Chef. Always."

Sometimes a girl just likes to be treated like a chicken.

classic roast chicken with herb butter   SERVES 4

3 tablespoons unsalted butter, softened

2 teaspoons herbes de Provence

1 (3½- to 4-pound) whole chicken

1½ teaspoons kosher salt

1 teaspoon freshly ground black pepper

1 small bunch fresh thyme

4 smashed and peeled garlic cloves

1 Preheat the oven to 400°F. In a small bowl, mash together the butter and herbes de Provence. Pat the chicken completely dry with paper towels so that the butter will slide easily along its skin. Massage the chicken inside and out with salt and pepper. Thrust the thyme and garlic deep into the cavity of the chicken.

2 Fill your hand with herb butter and gently slide your fingers beneath the skin of the breast, slathering butter on the flesh. Work your way down to the thighs. Rub additional butter all over the surface of the skin.

3 Tightly truss the chicken according to the instructions on page 34. The tighter you truss her, the juicier she will be.

4 Place the chicken on a rack set over a rimmed baking sheet. Roast until the thigh juices run clear and the skin is golden, 1 hour to 1 hour and 15 minutes. Cover with foil and let rest 20 minutes before carving.

Epilogue

MEET SHIFTY BLADES

What the fuck was I thinking? The world isn't ready for full-on radish cuisine. The radish granita was a hit, but the radish-tini is just too far ahead of its time. Well, one day it will be recognized as a classic. Until then, I'd better get my shit together for the cookbook proposal I'm supposed to write.

As I open the fridge I'm nearly bowled over as a pink cannonball plunges from the top shelf and hits the floor with a dull splat. I roll my eyes and suppress my irritation at this needless disruption in my kitchen.

What's a chicken doing in my refrigerator anyway? Mrs. Smith is getting careless in her housekeeping. I'll have to talk to her about following my ingredients lists more precisely. Must I write everything out in capital letters?

I pick up the fallen bird, and push the giblets bag back into her cavity. What a mess. But fuck, look at that skin. It's perfect. Nearly as pink as the radish. Yes, I must confess, she is an alluring little piece. There might be something I could do with this bird. I imagine what the bite of my new oven would do to that skin—crisp it up beautifully, I suspect. Oh man. *Get a grip, Chef. You've got work to do.*

I start prepping out some herbs, but the blush on that chicken keeps drawing my eye, almost as if it were pulsing. Nobody's making great art with chicken, but it might be fun to play around. Which knife, I wonder? The santoku would certainly bring her to heel. But the vintage carbon-steel French chef's knife would be more pleasurable. Or the steely discipline of the Wüsthof? That rack truly holds a knife for my every mood.

"Yes, quite a collection," I say aloud. It suddenly occurs to me that this beautiful chicken is like a virgin block of marble, just waiting for a sculptor's tools to elevate it above the everyday. This bird's delicious, glowing shade of pink seems to want to prove to me that a real artist, one with finesse, technique, and a good knife, could make a transcendent chicken.

"I couldn't agree more," I mumble to myself, impressed by my own idea. I count my knives to calm myself. "Fifty blades, to be precise. This kitchen is my domain. I need to have complete control when I prep."

I realize I've been talking to myself, so I may as well talk to the chicken. I remember Julia used to do that on her show. My television babysitter as a child. I remember the constant smell of Tater Tots. *Fucking hell.*

I don't want to repeat the whole radish experience. Am I ready to take on a new Ingredient, something as humdrum as chicken? How do you finesse chicken? I groan inwardly at all the possibilities this presents. Well, getting there is going to be half the fun.

"It's all about finesse, Miss Hen." *Christ, I'm lecturing a fucking chicken.* "I have enormous respect for food. To derive deep satisfaction from the mundane: tournéing a radish, cutting a potato, portioning a syllabub. These form the foundation of what I do."

A syllabub? I might be losing my marbles. But the chicken draws me onward with her ravishing skin. Everything about this humble, exquisite bird points to how the ordinary can be raised to the extraordinary. Through the disheveled plastic I can make out the curve of her perfect breast.

And there you have it. I have to come up with fifty recipes by next month, I'm talking to a chicken, and I have a hard-on.

Taters, Baby

*crispy roasted potatoes with
garlic and thyme* **SERVES 4**

Kosher salt

1½ pounds small Yukon
Gold potatoes

6 garlic cloves, smashed
but not peeled

3 tablespoons chicken fat,
olive oil, or peanut oil

Freshly ground black
pepper

6 thyme sprigs

1 Bring a pot of heavily salted water to a boil and
cook the potatoes until just tender, 15 to 25 minutes
depending upon how big they are. Drain and let cool.

2 Preheat the oven to 425°F. Use your hands to lightly
smash the potatoes. Toss the potatoes and garlic with
the chicken fat or oil and spread out on a rimmed
baking sheet. Season with more salt and pepper and
top with the thyme sprigs. Roast until golden brown all
over, 35 to 45 minutes. Serve with chicken.

Rival Radish Salad

*radish salad with cucumbers,
sesame, and ginger* **SERVES 4**

3 cups thinly sliced radishes
(from 1 bunch)

2 tablespoons finely
chopped chives

4 teaspoons sesame oil

2 teaspoons fresh lemon
juice

1½ teaspoons grated ginger

¾ teaspoon kosher salt

3 Kirby cucumbers, thinly
sliced

1 teaspoon soy sauce

1 Combine the radishes, chives, sesame oil, lemon juice,
ginger, and salt in a small bowl and toss to combine.
Let stand 5 minutes. In a separate bowl, toss the
cucumbers and soy sauce.

2 Mound the radishes in the center of a large platter and
place the cucumbers all around. Serve.

Beaten Chocolate Foam
bittersweet chocolate sabayon **SERVES 2 TO 4**

¼ cup sugar

⅓ cup ruby port

4 egg yolks

2 tablespoons unsweetened cocoa powder

Pinch of fine sea salt

Fresh raspberries, for serving

1 Bring a medium pot filled halfway with water to a simmer. In a heatproof bowl large enough to sit over (but not touch) the water, whisk together the sugar, port, egg yolks , cocoa, and salt.

2 Set the bowl over the simmering water and whisk constantly until the mixture is thick, foamy, and tripled in volume, about 5 minutes.

3 Fill serving dishes with berries and immediately spoon the sabayon over the top.

Hot Bird Cocktail
bourbon with rosemary syrup and lemon
SERVES 1

2 ounces bourbon, preferably 100-proof, such as Wild Turkey or Fighting Cock

1 teaspoon Rosemary Simple Syrup (see box)

Splash of Old Speckled Hen ale

Twist of lemon

Rosemary sprig, for garnish

Stir the bourbon and syrup with ice. Strain into a chilled rocks glass and add a splash of ale. Rub the rim of a glass with a lemon twist. Garnish with the twist and a rosemary sprig, or, optionally, a clean roasted chicken bone.

ROSEMARY SIMPLE SYRUP

In a small saucepan, heat ½ cup of sugar with ½ cup water and 2 tablespoons of roughly chopped rosemary needles. Simmer for 5 minutes, until the syrup thickens and the sugar dissolves. Let cool. Store in the refrigerator.

ACKNOWLEDGMENTS

THANK YOU to all the people who made this book possible.

First and foremost, many thanks to the Poultry Posse at Clarkson Potter: Doris Cooper, Erica Gelbard, Carly Gorga, Stephanie Huntwork, Pam Krauss, Donna Passannante, Jane Treuhaft, and Kate Tyler.

Thanks to the photography team responsible for the food porn—photographer and chicken wrangler John von Pamer and chicken stylist Michelli Knauer.

Thanks to Luke Guldan and Chris Roth for fab abs.

Finally, thank you to my understanding spouse, who claimed not to mind eating chicken every night for weeks, and put up with the endless "why did the chicken cross the road" jokes. (One answer: there was a racy cookbook on the other side.)

ABOUT THE AUTHOR

FL FOWLER is a pseudonym.

INDEX

Note: Page references in *italics* indicate photographs.